Leading School-based Networks

Schools hav————established history of working together but the persistent challenge of achieving e   and equity within education systems has renewed interest in generating context-spe   ttions through localised networks. As networking and collaboration have become mo   tream activities, they have raised new leadership challenges for existing school leade   rompted discussion about whether new types of leaders and leadership are required for   re.

Based ar   lifecycle of a network, *Leading School-based Networks* traces the development of a networ   ts initial inception, exploring the ways in which it can be sustained and remain capa   of meeting the future challenges faced by schools and their communities. The book explo   series of important issues facing school leaders, including:

- the bene   of investing time and energy in networks with other schools and communities;
- the pa   r problems faced by schools and the education system that are best tackled by netwo   d solutions;
- the ad   s for schools and communities of engaging with collaborative reform agenda;
- the wa   which networks can be managed, and the differences between leading a school or a te   and a network;
- the ele   ts that make an effective network.

The book   ds on UK and international research to discuss the development and leadership of networks   to outline a number of tried-and-tested leadership approaches. In addition, the authors dra   their own experience and research to provide accounts of real networks and expose the   es of networking. Each chapter addresses a key leadership issue and ends with a series of t   to help those who are leading and facilitating networks tackle these in practice.

This boc   ill be of interest to practising school leaders, network coordinators, public sector officers, postgraduate students and those researching educational leadership and school improvement.

Mark Hadfield is Professor in Applied and Practitioner Research at the School of Education, University of Wolverhampton, UK.

Christopher Chapman is Reader in Educational Leadership and School Improvement, University of Manchester, UK.

DISCARD

B.S.U.C. - LIBRARY

00283787

DISCARD

Leading
School-based
Networks

Mark Hadfield and
Christopher Chapman

 Routledge
Taylor & Francis Group

LONDON AND NEW YORK

First published 2009
by Routledge
2 Park Square, Milton Park, Abingdon, Oxon OX14 4RN

Simultaneously published in the USA and Canada
by Routledge
270 Madison Ave, New York, NY 10016

Routledge is an imprint of the Taylor & Francis Group, an informa business

© 2009 Mark Hadfield and Christopher Chapman

Typeset in Garamond by
Swales & Willis Ltd, Exeter, Devon
Printed and bound in Great Britain by
TJ International Ltd, Padstow, Cornwall

All rights reserved. No part of this book may be reprinted or reproduced
or utilised in any form or by any electronic, mechanical, or other means,
now known or hereafter invented, including photocopying and recording,
or in any information storage or retrieval system, without permission in
writing from the publishers.

British Library Cataloguing in Publication Data
A catalogue record for this book is available from the British Library

Library of Congress Cataloging in Publication Data
Hadfield, Mark.
  Leading school-based networks/Mark Hadfield and Christopher Chapman.
      p. cm.
  Includes bibliographical references and index.
  1. Inter-school cooperation–Great Britain.   2. School management and
organization–Great Britain.   3. School improvement programs–Great Britain.
4. Educational leadership–Great Britain.   I. Chapman, Christopher, 1972–   II. Title.
  LB2901.H33 2009
  371.2–dc22   2008044830

ISBN10: 0–415–46464–1 (hbk)
ISBN10: 0–415–46465–X (pbk)
ISBN10: 0–203–87900–7 (ebk)

ISBN13: 979-0-415-46464-2 (hbk)

BATH SPA UNIVERSITY
NEWTON PARK LIBRARY

Class No.	
371.2 HAD	
PD	7/12/09

Contents

Illustrations

Figures

Tables

Preface

This book draws on our 20 years of experience of working within, and with, a wide range of school-based networks. During this time we have taken on a variety of roles including as practitioners and leaders within networked-based projects, acting as external facilitators, researching, evaluating their impact and advising policy makers on the possibilities and pitfalls of a networking approach. We first started supporting and researching collaboration between schools in the 1990s when competition-based policies were at the height of their 'popularity' and collaboration between schools was pragmatically difficult. So unusual was any form of formalised or substantive collaboration between secondary schools in many of the regions we worked that we tended to conceptualise these networks as 'localised counter-policies'. Now collaboration between schools is very much in vogue and being part of a network of schools in many education systems across the world means running with the tide of central government policy rather than against it. It would seem that to network has become the orthodoxy rather than a minority activity.

Although networks are often described as 'messy' and 'complex', this book is based around a simple design flow for a school network. This flow, from purpose to structure, also involves discussing the kinds of capacities required at different levels of a network and the sorts of processes needed to cohere and develop them. Working through this design process is of relevance to those just starting to plan their networks and experienced networkers alike. If you are thinking about how to evaluate a current network, struggling with issues around sustainability or keen to improve the leadership in your network, these areas are considered in detail in the later chapters of the book.

The first chapter of the book provides a basic framework for thinking about what a school network is and why people get involved in networks. After this introduction to networks, and the benefits of networking, the book moves on to issues of design and the challenges of establishing a network. The middle chapters then consider the linked issues of building leadership capacity and the sustainability of networks. A whole chapter is also devoted to the challenge of harnessing the power of an external facilitator and how this can be optimised by network leaders. The final chapter then considers the future of school networks and collaboratives by picking out key trends and extrapolating these into three near-future scenarios.

The ethos that underpins this book is that when used carefully school-to-school collaboration can be a powerful approach not only supporting schools and improving the education they offer to their pupils, but also changing the very nature of education systems themselves. In this sense, we are optimistic about the power of networks and their potential to support systemic change. However, this is not a naive optimism; we are very aware of the limitations of networks and networking, we have direct experience of poorly designed, cynically motivated and ineptly led networks. We have experienced 'empty networks' where on the surface there seems to be powerful action, however, on closer examination there is little if anything of substance occurring, except for the drawing down of resources from an external agency. If though we were pushed to declare our position with regard to school-to-school networking it would resonate strongly with the following quote from a headteacher: 'I wanted to join this network because I really believed it was going to make the biggest difference to children.' It is in this spirit we offer this book.

Mark Hadfield
Christopher Chapman
October 2008

Acknowledgements

We would like to thank all the members of the Network Learning Group (NLG) without whose efforts and support we would never have become so immersed in the world of school networks. In particular we would like to thank members of the leadership and research team including David Jackson, Jasbir Mann, Michael Jopling, Michelle Anderson, Chris Kubiak, Barbara Spender, Chris Noden and Ronnie Woods. Furthermore, we are also indebted to our colleagues within the school effectiveness and improvement communities who have supported our efforts and inspired our thinking over the past decades. We are particularly grateful to Mel Ainscow, Christopher Day, Alma Harris, David Hopkins, Dave Reynolds and Mel West for their invaluable insights and critical friendship.

Chapter 1

Why get involved in a network of schools?

Introduction

This chapter sets out to answer two linked questions:

• What do we mean by a 'network of schools'?
• Why should schools and school leaders spend time and energy getting involved in them?

In this first chapter we only give a brief description of what we mean by a school network. Our aim is to introduce you to the key ideas that will be developed in later chapters when we discuss how to design, establish, lead and sustain a network of schools. At this point though we do attempt a much fuller answer to our second question.

We have written this book from a particular perspective as to what constitutes school networks, which is that they need to be primarily educational endeavours entered into voluntarily by staff and pupils. Different forms of networks, collaboratives and federations have become an established part of many educational landscapes and have arisen for a number of reasons. Some have been 'imposed' on schools, others have been 'incentivised' by the offer of external funding, but many have arisen because of the efforts of educational leaders who want to make a difference in their locality. In this book we are concerned with the latter group; that is school networks whose primary agenda is to improve the educational offer to those involved, rather than resource alliances seeking funding or political collectives trying to influence others.

Our emphasis on volunteerism is important because if networks place learning of both pupils and staff at their heart, it requires active participation for this to be empowering, not enforced or coerced engagement. Network theorists have long argued that what distinguishes networks from other organisational forms is the nature of participation exhibited by their members:

> Participation is at the core of what makes a network different from other organizational or process forms. Who participates (issues around power,

and resources), how they participate (issues about relationships, coordination, facilitation, governance), why they participate (issues around vision, values, needs, benefits, motivation, commitment), and for how long (issues around sustainability).

(Church *et al.*, 2002, p. 14)

In stressing volunteerism we do not wish to appear overly idealistic and we recognise that individuals will have pragmatic reasons for joining a school network as well as moral, and what we might call, political motivations. This means that in terms of building a network we need to answer pragmatic questions about 'Why should I get involved?' as well as appealing to more idealistic motivations.

In this chapter we therefore consider the evidence that networks 'work'. By this we mean that they appear to meet the needs of pupils and staff within schools. This means trying to answer questions such as: What evidence is there that networks and networking benefit pupils, schools and local communities? What does this evidence reveal about what networks appear to be good at? We then finish the chapter with a broader discussion of the moral and political reasons why some leaders and many practitioners have invested their, and their schools', energies in working collaboratively with others.

What are these things called networks of schools?

Much has been written about what constitutes a 'network', and it is clear that the term can mean very different things to different people. The *Oxford English Dictionary* describes a network as 'a group or system of interconnected people or things'. Hence, at one level the word can be used to refer to a group of connected computers, and at another a complex web of professional and social relationships between people and organisations. The sheer plasticity of the term 'network' means that it has been applied to a wide range of social and technological phenomena.

Similarly in education the term 'network' has been applied to professional networks of individuals that can span a local area or whole country (Little, 1993; Lieberman and Grolnick, 1996), or networks of personal relationships within a single school (Bryk *et al.*, 1999). Even when applied specifically to networks of schools it can appear that it is applied to groups of schools with very different foci. For example, Priscilla Wohlstetter (2003) in her study of Los Angeles networks focuses on the role of joint problem solving in drawing schools together into networks:

A network . . . is a group of organisations working together to solve problems or issues of mutual concern that are too large for any one organisation to handle on its own (Mandell, 1999). Applied to schools, the idea of networks suggests that schools working together in a collaborative effort would be more effective in enhancing organisational capacity and improving student learning than individual schools working on their own (Wohlstetter and Smith, 2000).

(Wohlstetter *et al.*, 2003, p. 399)

Unsurprisingly, when the Organisation for Economic Cooperation and Development (OECD) Lisbon Seminar (2003) attempted to define 'Networked Learning Communities' as they built on the research into professional learning communities, they placed emphasis on knowledge transfer, professional learning and their position between central and local educational structures:

> Networked Learning Communities are purposefully led social entities that are characterised by a commitment to quality, rigour and a focus on outcomes . . .. They promote the dissemination of good practice, enhance the professional development of teachers, support capacity building in schools, mediate between centralised and decentralised structures, and assist in the process of re-structuring and re-culturing educational organisational systems.
>
> (OECD, 2003, p. 154)

We do not want to add to the very long list of definitions, rather our approach is to argue that all networks share a set of common features: structures, interactions (processes), agency and purposes. We then use these characteristics to define what we mean by a network of schools by discussing how they are both similar to and different from being part of social or informal professional networks. Making this differentiation is illuminating because anyone working in a school is already probably part of several such networks, based on connections with individuals with whom they share a professional or personal enthusiasm, with colleagues from previous schools they have worked in, to people they have met at professional development events or as part of their initial training. We want to argue that becoming part of a formal network of schools is a quantum leap on from being part of an informal professional network, and making this leap requires a good understanding of networks and how they operate.

Structures

Network structures are probably the most popular way of distinguishing networks from other organisational forms. A range of metaphors has been used from the technological to the more organic to describe the 'net' part of a network. One of our favourites was developed by Church *et al.* (2002) who used a 'fisherman's net' metaphor (see Figure 1.1) to describe the structure of a network of individuals. A fisherman's net is based on threads that are knotted together. In a network of individuals the 'threads' that link people together,

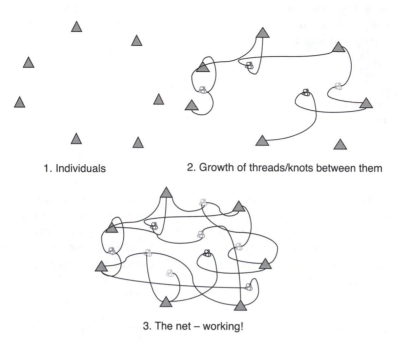

1. Individuals

2. Growth of threads/knots between them

3. The net – working!

Figure 1.1 Network knots and threads
Source: Church *et al.* (2002, p. 16)

and represent the 'soft' part of the network structure, are the relationships, communications and trust that link people. The 'knots' provide the 'harder' part of the structure and are the activities that bring people in the network together, meetings and events or even video-conferencing or instant messaging sessions. The 'net' attains its structural strength from the interaction of these two components.

What is important about Church's metaphor is that it stresses the interaction of the soft, the relational structures that bring people together, along with the operational, the meetings etc. This is important as all networks have some form of structure that brings people together and organises the connections between them. What provides this structure, and the patterns of interactions that result, have been used as means of classifying different types of networks. Even social networks, or systems, require some form of structure to maintain them:

> Social systems involve regularized relations of interdependence between individuals or groups, that typically can be best analysed as recurrent social practices. Social systems are systems of social interaction . . . Systems in this terminology, have structures, or, more accurately, have structural

properties. Structures are necessarily (logically) properties of systems or collectives.

(Giddens cited in Callinicos, 1987, p. 40)

Within social systems these 'regularized relationships' and 'recurrent social patterns' can be brought about by structures as simple as supporting a football club or visiting the same coffee shop. Formalised professional networks are built around different sorts of structures. The soft structures that operate in social networks are important, such as trust and knowledge of each other, but in a school network they are supplemented by professional purposes and motivations, for example, by a joint problem or shared professional aim. Similarly the knots that hold these threads in place are a different sort of activity or event, such as planning meetings, working groups or cross-school research teams. It is the interaction of these 'hard' and 'soft' structures that create the potential for focusing and harnessing the energy and passion of those in the network.

School networks also require structures that interact with, and between, the internal school structures that organise what happens within individual schools. These structures, such as network conferences, cross-school meetings and inter-visitations provide the means to develop the 'soft' aspects of the network structure that bring people together, the professional relationships, while at the same time creating the 'hard' structures, the knots that provide the opportunity for joint working and effective collaboration.

Interactions (processes)

Whenever people in a network come together, some form of interaction takes place. In social networks such interactions may be little more than amiable conversations around a shared interest or experience. These interactions can become more complex exchanges as individuals swap expert knowledge about a hobby, exchange local knowledge about good places to eat and barter goods and services. Social networks are often marked out by this multiplicity of interactions, each arising out of sets of individual interests. In contrast professional networks are marked by more limited sets of interactions based on specifically designed processes aimed at achieving professional rather than social outcomes. It is the nature of these processes, and the intentions behind them, that distinguishes a school network from a social one.

The kinds of processes that occur within school networks will range from shared learning experiences, through joint professional development activities, and joint working, such as planning together, to undertaking collaborative change, such as working on curriculum innovations and practitioner enquiry. Other processes, such as leadership and management activities will interlink this joint working to coordinate it and ensure it impacts on the classroom. A network of schools will therefore have within it not only the kinds of interactions that one might find in a social network but also specifically designed learning and coordinating processes.

Networked agency

The third difference between social and professional networks is in the balance between the degree of collective and individual agency that their members exhibit, a balance we have termed networked agency. In social networks there may be relatively little shared understanding of what is occurring in the different parts of a network, and only limited commitment to any form of collective activity. This is not to say that social networks do not get involved in collective action, as evidenced by the numerous social events and fund raisers organised by them, but they do not require this in order to function as a network. In contrast, for a professional network to be termed such there needs to be a shared commitment to a degree of collective action aimed at achieving explicit professional goals. If this element is not present within networks then a number of things can happen. They can become 'talking shops' in which professionals come together and enact little more than what occurs within social networks. Or the networks will act more like a professional 'club' in which a minority of activists provide various 'services' for the passive majority. Remember it is the nature of the participation of its members that gives a network its unique organisational characteristics, and 'talking shops' and 'clubs', although forms of networking, are not networks of schools.

Purposes

The final characteristic of all networks is that people come together for a purpose, or more accurately a range of purposes. A crude differentiator between social networks and networks of schools is that the latter generally espouse an 'official' collective aim, as shown by the following:

> We expect, by the end of the programme, all schools to have introduced strategies and activities that will develop their institutions as being emotionally literate and this will impact significantly on pupils' attainments. The intention is to link the development of emotional intelligence to all our activities for both pupils and staff.
>
> (Janus Network of Schools, 2005)

This form of explicitly stated collective purpose is of a very different form and scale to the individual needs that are likely to be fulfilled by being part of social network, such as having fun, meeting others etc. This makes them a crude means of differentiating between types of networks because it would involve juxtaposing the espoused 'official' collective aims of a school network with the individual needs of members of a social network. A more sophisticated analysis is to consider if there are different types of individual purposes between why people participate within school and social networks, while still recognising that teachers might well be meeting social as well as professional needs by participating in such networks.

Both social and professional networks play a part in the process of identity formation. So any discussion of the purposes behind peoples' decisions to participate in a school network needs to recognise the role it can play, through their interactions within it, in the process of creating, building and giving meaning to their professional identity. Prophets tend not to be recognised in their own home land and innovative practitioners can often become over looked in their own schools. A network may give them a degree of recognition, even if this was not the original motivation or purpose of them getting involved. Similarly networks based on subject specialists have been shown to be particularly effective in part because of the shared professional identity, as for example geography teachers, that already exists in such groupings and also because this identity is validated and valued within such networks.

Individual involvement in collaborative work often gives people the opportunity to engage in professional activities that they would not necessarily have access to in their own school. This might be a relatively self-centred motivation, for example it may give them the chance to take on a leadership role that they would not normally be given in their own school and thus help them develop their careers. Similarly a network might create a big enough group of practitioners interested in a specific area to make it economically viable to provide them with specially tailored professional development activities.

The individual purposes that shape peoples' participation in a school network are likely to be as diverse and complex as those that mark our involvement in other forms of networking, to an extent they are distinguishable by the fact that they will generally have a more 'professional' focus. Instrumentally people get involved in networks to access support, information and to keep abreast of new developments and initiatives. But the major difference is that individual participation within a professional network will require them explicitly, or implicitly, to articulate their own espoused agenda for taking part and be comfortable with being challenged both directly, and indirectly, by what they do collectively. In reality the individual 'purposes' that drive forward participation in a network of schools are going to range from the somewhat instrumental, the chance to do things not available to them professionally elsewhere, to the more abstract and idealistic.

These four key features of networks, the structures that bring people together, the nature of the interactions between them, the degree of networked agency that exists and the purposes behind individuals' involvement, all help us define what we mean by a school network. This is a powerful model because it can not only help us understand what the key factors are that shape the individual experience of being part of a school network, but can also at a global level assist us to analyse and judge the effectiveness and sustainability of a network. For example, recognising that the motivations to participate in a network range from the need to find somewhere where one 'belongs' professionally to creating a space where one might be given the chance to try out new ideas and take risks is the first step in understanding how these need to be managed and challenged.

What evidence is there that being in a network of schools benefits pupils, schools and local communities?

Before we start to dive too deeply into the existing research base around networks of schools, it is important to raise a note of caution. As we will discover in later chapters the term network not only covers a wide range of connections between groups of schools, it has also been rather loosely applied to various instances of schools working together. What this means is that when reviewing the evidence of any potential benefits it is hard to differentiate networks from various other forms of collaboratives, partnerships, alliances and consortia. In our search for evidence of the impact of school networks we have therefore adopted, and slightly adapted, the expansive definition used by the reviewers whom to-date have carried out the only systematic review of the impact of school networks on pupils: 'Groups or systems of interconnected people and/or organisations (including schools) whose aims and purposes include the improvement of learning, [or learning opportunities], and whose structure and organisation include explicit strategies designed to achieve these aims' (Bell *et al.*, 2006, p. 21).

Our addition of the phrase 'or learning opportunities' in the above definition is to highlight that in this analysis there are networks whose focus is on the provision of additional services, extended provision or new educational opportunities for learners rather than aiming for generic academic improvement or the targeting of specific curriculum innovations.

A final cautionary note relates to the issue of causality, in this case how to link any network activity to a specific impact within a classroom, school or local community. As is discussed in detail later, networks have infrastructures based on webs of connections through which a wide variety of interactions take place. This means it is highly problematic to follow the impact of any network activity through these multiple connections and interactions and then claim that what takes place in a specific lesson arose because of something that occurred months ago during a joint school development session. Add to this problem that there might be several network-based interactions occurring at a variety of connection points within a network at any one time, some of which will be vital to a particular innovation's success while others are tangential or make no real contribution, and one can see the difficult task that both researchers and practitioners have in assessing the effectiveness of any network. It is therefore perhaps not surprising, considering how difficult it is to identify any kind of causal chain within a network, that although anecdotal claims of their impact on schools abound in a wide variety of evaluations, practitioner accounts articulating the specific impacts of networking are more problematic.

A common theme that runs through these accounts is the discussion of how networks impact throughout a school affecting both its leader, staff, pupils and even parents and local communities:

> Although many schools found evaluating the academic impacts of the initiative a challenging task, the work impacted in a variety of forms, such as staff becoming more aware and reflective about their practice, and learners working in more positive learning environments. In a majority of schools these kinds of developments were also reported to be reflected in improved academic achievements.
>
> (Rudd *et al.*, 2004, p. 43)

At one level this discussion of multiple effects complicates any truly causal analysis but it does give general support to the idea that networks actually impact on pupils and schools. It does this because one would expect to see a range of interim or 'proxy' indicators of network effects on pupils, such as changes to teachers' attitudes, knowledge and practice. In the following review of the evidence we explore this idea of networks having multiple levels of impact within school.

The evidence that school networks impact on pupils

Possibly the strongest evidential basis that networks impact upon pupil achievement is provided by Bell *et al*'s (2006) systematic review of schools networks from 1995–2005. As already discussed this review took a broad definition of what constituted a network but came to the following conclusion on reviewing some 119 studies before focusing in on some 19 international studies, and categorising them as having high to low levels of impact:

> Eleven studies investigated and reported pupil impact. . . . We found six studies where the networks' impact on pupil attainment and/or achievement and engagement was high. Five of these were targeted at improvements for SEN [special educational needs], at risk or minority students. Attainment gains included significant improvements in pupil progression and employment rates, overall public test score increases, increased academic achievement in core subject gains for project students in reading, language and mathematics. . . . Two studies were found to have medium attainment impact. In one, the network narrowed the gap between minority and non-minority students and between economically disadvantaged and non-disadvantaged pupils. The other found student achievements were mixed, but included a 'steady increase' in performance

in maths and science; steady improvement in grade scores on non verbal tests and an increase in students' reflection and responsibility for their work. In terms of achievement and engagement one study found greater pupil involvement in school clubs and after-school activities; an increase in pupil self-confidence and self esteem, an improved attitude to school and increased attendance.

(Bell *et al.*, 2006, p. 52)

What this systematic review highlighted was that in terms of measurable outcomes on pupil achievement, unsurprisingly, the more effective networks had more specific and narrower aims and targeted their efforts on particular groups of pupils. To what extent this finding arises because it is much easier to measure the impact on smaller groups of pupils is beyond the scope of a systematic review. What can be deduced is that in part these outcomes came about because of the nature of the projects included. A significant proportion of these were focused on groups of pupils with specific needs or who required a level and kind of support that was difficult for certain schools in isolation to offer, such as the most socially excluded or underachieving students. The review highlights how in some cases it would have been difficult to see how these impacts could have been achieved without a network. What was apparent was that certain schools struggling with intractable social and educational issues benefited from working in a network. Part of the success was due to how networks of schools were more able to mobilise a wide range of resources and expertise, often in short supply when dealing with parents and local community groups.

Is there evidence, though, of networks impacting more broadly than on the most excluded of pupils? Within the UK there has been a number of networking initiatives funded by central government. They have tended to be focused at the two ends of the achievement spectrum, and have ranged from providing support mechanisms to underachieving schools to trying to harness the expertise and capacity of successful schools. Again the most robust evidence, because of the pressure to provide funders with evidence of impact, lies within those studies that have targeted inner city pupils. Our recent review of 17 different UK networks working in a mixture of inner city and complex and challenging circumstances (Hadfield and Jopling, 2007) led to the following conclusion:

The pupil impact evidence in the case studies, and the broader reviews, supports the argument that well-led and appropriately structured collaboration between schools facing complex and challenging circumstances helped their leaders to balance short term pressures to improve pupil attainment with long term desires to improve the educational experiences of their pupils and the engagement of their communities.

(Hadfield and Jopling, 2007, p. 3)

This review identified evidence of global improvements in attainment across whole networks at both primary and secondary level. Even within those networks that showed such global improvements, variations in rates of improvement between collaborating schools were often apparent. These variations not only reflected the dynamic and unpredictable contexts they worked in but also shifts in the internal capacities of schools that affected their ability to benefit from any collaborative activities, an issue discussed in more detail in Chapter 5. The conclusion also reflected that there was evidence in several networks that collaboration supported schools taking the 'risk' of investing in long-term improvements, rather than going for short-term gains.

Unsurprisingly then, the most significant benefits were in those areas, and also in dealing with the issues, to paraphrase Mandell (1999), that individual schools find difficult to do on their own. Both these reviews seem to indicate that a network-based approach should be considered when individual schools lack the resources or expertise to overcome a particular challenge, when they face an issue that is too large to deal with on their own or they face a challenge that is based within the relationships between schools and local communities. The most recent wave of network-based initiatives in the UK has arisen in part because of the challenges set out by the Every Child Matters agenda and the need to provide better vocational education opportunities requiring schools to become part of multi-agency and cross-phase networks.

Three of the networks reviewed by Hadfield and Jopling (2007) demonstrated another potential impact on schools: an enhanced ability to manage short-term improvement in pupil attainment and achievement alongside longer term capacity building and large-scale curriculum innovation.

Vignette: simultaneous improvement and innovation

The performance data (Figure 1.2) from the four primary schools in this network (it also included one secondary school), demonstrated a history of low attainment compared to other schools in the local authority, and very low compared to all schools nationally.

While this trend continued in 2003, the end of the first full year of collaborative activity, it was reversed in 2004 when three of the four schools exceeded the local authority's average attainment figures (Figure 1.3) and two of them (including a school where 44.2 per cent of the standard assessment tasks (SATs) cohort had SEN) also exceeded national averages. In terms of value added this improvement was even more remarkable.

At the same time as achieving these improvements in pupil achievement, this collaborative undertook a massive and systematic change in its approach to learning and teaching as they introduced more inclusive and creative curricula, focusing in on pupils' learning. These were innovations that aimed

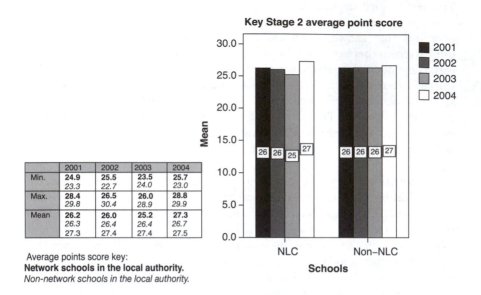

Average points score key:
Network schools in the local authority.
Non-network schools in the local authority.

	2001	2002	2003	2004
Min.	**24.9**	**25.5**	**23.5**	**25.7**
	23.3	*22.7*	*24.0*	*23.0*
Max.	**28.4**	**26.5**	**26.0**	**28.8**
	29.8	*30.4*	*28.9*	*29.9*
Mean	**26.2**	**26.0**	**25.2**	**27.3**
	26.3	*26.4*	*26.4*	*26.7*
	27.3	*27.4*	*27.4*	*27.5*

Figure 1.2 Performance data of four schools in one network over four years

to boost pupils' confidence and engagement in their learning and to create the possibility of longer term gains in achievement.

Another example of simultaneous improvement came from one of the longest enduring collaboratives reviewed in the case studies. This was a group of 11 secondary schools that had come together in 1997 in response to perceived shortcomings in local authority provision. It had improved attainment across all the schools with GCSE 5A*–C results between 2001 and 2005 rising significantly faster than the local rate. This has been achieved at the same time as it has made significant impacts in the areas of exclusion and their curriculum on offer. Rather than attempting a quick fix by removing problem pupils from school, the collaborative set a target of zero permanent exclusions. One of the headteachers involved explicitly links this to the partnership's developing sense of collective responsibility in which 'the good thing is that nobody, as in the bad old days, can just boot some one out'. Growing trust and shared information amongst the schools enabled them to identify one school that was excluding pupils more readily than the others and they changed its policy. The result was greater consistency of practice and a direct impact on pupils' experiences of education. The collaborative went on to draw down local authority funding to provide enhanced support to pupils at risk of exclusion. The collaborative also worked to enhance vocational education provision, partly dealing with the causes of pupil non-participation and drop-out.

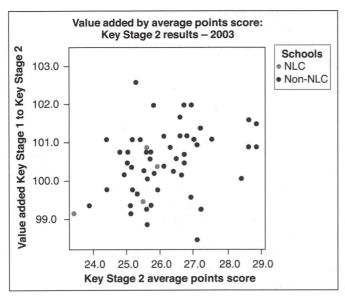

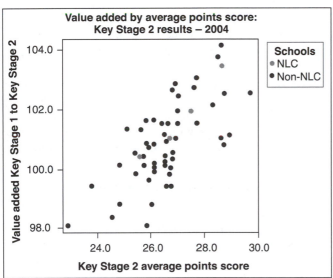

Figure 1.3 Pupil performance data of network and non-network schools (2003 and 2004)

These case studies provided evidence that effective networks could help schools improve standards and increase their capacity to innovate and be creative. This appeared to be because in such circumstances a network could act as part 'defence mechanism' by helping them resist external pressure to improve based on inappropriately designed or relative ineffective 'generic' strategies. This resistance was in part based on their ability as a network to identify and use approaches that they saw being effective in similar schools to their own, even in some instances from within their own network.

A network can also act as a 'store' of capacity and resources, allowing individual schools to draw down additional help when they need it and more importantly when they can make best use of it, rather than it being determined by the schedule of some external funding body. Although in some networks certain 'high capacity' schools might be the major store of resources, in others, particularly as the foci of the network changes, it is not unusual to see different schools taking on this role.

In summary, both internationally and nationally there is evidence of networks having an impact upon pupil achievement and attainment but much of the 'hard' evidence is limited to the most targeted and heavily funded initiatives within inner city schools.

An effective network can not only support individual schools to take on challenges they might find too daunting alone but also helps them balance competing external and internal agendas. It can do this in part by providing a support structure that will help them resist the imposition of inappropriate improvement strategies from outside while simultaneously acting as a resource bank of ideas and capacity. These characteristics of networks appear particularly important in schools in complex and challenging circumstances where many schools find themselves experiencing very wide fluctuations in their internal capacity, particularly, for example, when they suffer high staff turnover.

The evidence that school networks impact on teachers

Probably because of the emphasis on professional learning communities that permeates much of the North American literature, it is within accounts of national initiatives such as the Annenberg Challenge (Reyes and Phillips, 2002), district-based initiatives such as the British Columbia Network of Performance Based Schools and professional networks such as the National Writing Project that we can find some of the richest descriptions of how networks impact on teachers' knowledge, beliefs and classroom practices. Indeed as far back as 1996 Lieberman and Grolnick in their study of 16 US educational reform networks were commenting:

> We found that these networks were attempting to shift the meaning of adult learning away from prescription towards challenging involvement

and problem solving. They tried to achieve goals of participant learning and professional competence by modelling different modes of inquiry, supporting the formations of teams to create and write school-based plans for change, finding mechanisms to encourage cross-role groups to work together, focussing deeply on particular topics, and inviting the participants to help shape the agenda in their own terms.

(Lieberman and Grolnick, 1996, p. 9)

Improvements to the professional development experiences of teachers involved in networking arise from a number of factors. This is not least in part because of the opportunities they offer to teachers to work with other teachers outside of their school. On the whole teachers rate highly the opportunity to connect with others working in similar contexts with the same sorts of pupils. A recent MORI poll (MORI, 2004) asked teachers: 'To what extent, if at all would you say that collaboration between your school and others leads to an improvement in the motivation of teachers and other staff?' The response was that nearly a third, 28 per cent, replied 'A great deal' with just under half, 47 per cent, stating 'A fair amount'.

The impacts of school networks on practitioners arise not just because they find it motivating to connect with others outside of their school, it also seems to improve the overall quality of the professional development on offer. The evidence that networks provide improved professional development opportunities is spread throughout numerous evaluations and research accounts. The major benefits for staff of these changes can be drawn together into three main themes:

- improved access to local, national and international expertise;
- enhanced ability to innovate and enquire into one's own practice;
- supporting and structuring professional development opportunities so they result in changes to classroom practice.

Improved access to expertise might be as low key and specific as arranging for 'opportunities for sharing good practice with subject specialists in neighbouring schools' (OfSTED, 2003) to a high profile international expert launching a school-wide reform activity. By creating economies of scale, networks make it economically viable to hire in external expertise. They can also provide the structures that bring together groups of practitioners and provide the facilitation they need to learn from each other's insights and understandings.

Networks are fertile grounds for developing practitioner innovation and enquiry into their own practices, and just as importantly the practice of others in the network. This ability can also operate at a number of levels. In numerous instances school and teacher networks have been constructed around partnership with universities or forms of 'intermediary organisations' (McLaughlin and

Talbert, 2006) that have provided formal training and on-going support to practitioner research and enquiry. For example the Bay Area Schools Reform Collaborative in the US has over the last ten years been supporting 'Cycles of Inquiry' amongst its networks of 87 Leadership Schools (CRC, 2002). In a less formalised manner many networks are based around learning from each other's best practice and approaches to innovation. This may simply consist of a network organising monthly 'Bring and Brag' sessions where teachers meet after school to share new curriculum ideas or they may produce sophisticated network web portals and publications. A network's ability to transfer new practices out from individual practitioner researchers and enquiry groups and into classrooms across the network can also exert a strong cultural influence: 'The main reaction [to the research consortium] was one of enthusiasm . . . with particular regard to . . . awakening interest of colleagues and the growth of staffroom discussion about pedagogical issues – a talking culture previously absent' (MSSC, 2006, p. 8).

The final and possibly most significant impact on staff of being involved in a network is that it helps convert new professional learning into new practices. Networks appear to be able to do this because they simultaneously improve the quality of professional development and support the transfer of knowledge and practice. The argument here is threefold:

- First, networks can provide not only a wider professional development offer but also one that has more meaning for staff and is more likely to meet their needs and this greatly improves the chance of them making changes to classroom practice.
- Second, networks structures and processes can underpin those forms of collaborative professional development that have been shown to be particularly effective in terms of effecting classroom change.
- Third, networks can create a critical mass of activity that sustains innovation and widespread change across numerous classrooms and schools.

Let's quickly look at the evidence that underpins each of these claims, which lies not just within the research around networks but also in the wider professional development literature.

The evidence that certain forms of networks can substantially improve a practitioner's engagement within their own profession development is spread across the research on networks, from the evaluation of the Network Learning Programme in the UK (Sammons *et al.*, 2007) to the National Writing Project in the US (Lieberman and Wood, 2004). Working with others in a network has also been shown to provide greater opportunities for self and collective reflection on practice (Deloitte and Touche, 2000) and tends to increase engagement with more challenging and interactive forms of professional learning (Lieberman and Grolnick, 1996). All of which is set within the broad base of evidence of networking's ability to enhance morale and reduce professional isolation (Hopkins, 2000; Toole and Louis, 2002; Sliwka, 2003).

This improved engagement comes about for a range of reasons but vitally important is the voluntary nature of networking, which means that staff are more likely to opt into professional development opportunities that have strong personal and professional meaning.

The claim that networks support forms of collaborative continuing professional development (CPD) that have been shown to be particularly effective in changing classroom practices requires us to look at the broader literature. Some of the key characteristics of effective collaborative CPD have been identified in a recent systematic review carried out by the UK-based Evidence for Policy and Practice Information and Co-ordinating Centre (EPPI-Centre) (http://eppi.ioe.ac.uk/cms). This review identified seven common characteristics:

- 'the use of external expertise linked to school-based activity;
- observation;
- feedback (usually based on observation);
- an emphasis on peer support rather than leadership by supervisors;
- scope for teacher participants to identify their own CPD focus;
- processes to encourage, extend and structure professional dialogue;
- processes for sustaining the CPD over time to enable teachers to embed the practices in their own classroom settings'

(Cordingley *et al.*, 2003, p. 5).

Our argument is that although CPD within an individual school could demonstrate all of the above characteristics, networks facilitate the development of the majority of them. As has already been discussed networks can improve an individual's access to external expertise, similarly with their multitude of connections they provide opportunities for peer support, which may include observation and feedback from a wide range of joint working activities. The greater numbers of teachers involved in a network, and the capacity created by the pooling of resources, means that better defined groups of staff with similar interests and needs can be brought together and provided with more tailored support. Our own research within school networks has shown how staff often form semi-autonomous groups that meet over time and that encourage sustained professional dialogues and so assist members in implementing what they have recently learned (Hadfield, 2007).

The final claim is that networks are not only structures that support collaborative professional development but they also create and sustain a critical mass of activity that supports individual changes impact across numerous classrooms and schools. A number of factors within networks come together to enable innovations to go to scale. First, as we discuss later, the very nature of networks is that they often come together because of a shared professional issue or interest and so built into their fabric is a desire to learn from and with each other. These mutual aspirations form the basis of their ability to create a critical mass of activity that can take an innovation to scale.

This ability is further enhanced by the make-up of networks that bring together schools with different areas of expertise and capacities. Second, practitioners in networks that are based in a specific locality have the opportunity to learn from peers working in similar types of schools and working with 'their' sort of pupils. This is a situation that can overcome many of the cultural and psychological barriers to transferring new practices. Staff can see an innovation operating in situations akin to their own, and therefore are reassured about its feasibility. This can also raise staff and learners' expectations about what can be achieved in their 'context'. Networks, by linking staff with mutually similar aspirations, but with differing levels of expertise, and helping them to develop trust in each other, can also give individuals an increased sense of ownership of what they are learning. Rather than a change in classroom practice seemingly being imposed from outside, it quickly becomes something they feel that have ownership of. This sense of ownership, or as Coburn (2003) terms it 'transfer' of ownership, is key for a change to embed itself within practice.

Networks as structures can also help overcome a number of threats to the sustainability of any change. They can do this by quickly building 'internal' capacity within the network at various points so that the loss of a key individual does not stall a development. By acting as a 'reservoir' they can help overcome the problem of a short-term influx of resources and support that can quickly dissipate once external funders turn their attention to other issues and new priorities. A network can also sustain change by providing additional leadership capacity. School networks often create new 'middle' leadership roles, as discussed in more detail in Chapter 4, which are roles that sit between network and school structures and that try to ensure that network activity results in classroom change.

In the following quote we can see how one network used new leadership roles, two of which they termed 'Innovation Coordinators' and 'Knowledge Brokers', as a means of developing additional capacity while trying to ensure change happened within individual classrooms:

> Each school employs an Innovations Coordinator who organises teacher enquiry groups and network-wide learning days – e.g. a 'super learning day' on accelerated learning motivation. They also circulate resources around schools and 'roving displays'. The Knowledge Broker focuses on translating ideas into nitty-gritty action points for teachers. One admits that this does involve 'spoon-feeding' staff but feels that her work ensures the material is accessible to staff. Staff friendliness is important to ensure that not all activities are seen as add-ons for staff overloaded with work. The power of this approach is that it puts time and energy below the Headteacher level. The Headteachers have the vision and are excited about the network but don't have time to turn it into meaningful projects.

In summary, the evidence that networks impact positively upon staff can be found directly within the research and evaluation literature around networks but also indirectly in the broader literature concerned with collaborative professional development and the sustainability of educational reform. As with the evidence about pupil impact it reinforces the message that networks need to be effectively led, structured and organised around meaningful interactions. The rest of this book sets out to describe what such networks look like and how they can be created and sustained. Before moving on though, we want to finish our discussion about why people get involved in school networks by moving away from instrumental arguments about 'impact' and to consider reasons that encompass both professional values and political agendas.

Why get involved in networks? Professional values and political agendas

The 1990s was a decade in which, both in the UK and internationally, researchers and practitioners became increasingly aware of the negative outcomes of policies that had sought to use market forces and competition between schools to drive up standards in education. At this point the construct of collaboration in education was still mainly tied to discussions of the cultures within schools (Hargreaves, 1994; Hopkins and Lagerweij, 1996), a focus that arose in part because of the importance given to culture in the school improvement and professional development literature. It also reflected the status of school-to-school collaboratives at that time as relatively rare examples of 'counter-policies' to the dominant move towards competition and market-based policies. Such collaborations, at least in the UK, were often officially disapproved of by local and central government and as relatively uncommon phenomena were rarely studied.

By the end of the decade, as re-culturing began to be promoted to such an extent that it rivalled the importance of restructuring in the educational reform literature, Michael Fielding (1999) rightly lamented the instrumental tone that pervaded such discussions. The notion of promoting collaboration between peers had become an instrumental leadership tool to meet 'the particularities and idiosyncrasies of specific schools in specific circumstances'. For Fielding teachers' professionalism required them to stand outside of short-term and instrumental agendas:

> Teacher professionalism might be defined in terms of a commitment to the internal goals of learning and the maintenance of a critical distance between that practice and the external goods of schooling. Indeed, teachers might be seen as having a professional duty to adopt an explicitly oppositional stance to policies that prioritise the external goods of the institution or militate against the internal goods of learning; for

example, policies that are aimed at increasing competition, generating acquisitiveness or reproducing inequality.

(Fielding, 1999, p. 7)

Fielding argued that what was required was more than simple collaboration, as for him this often resulted in little more than instrumental partnerships within overly restricted foci on narrow sets of gains. Rather what was needed was

> [c]ollaboration within the context of a collegial relationship [as then it] is transformed from a narrowly functional activity circumscribed by instrumental rationality into a joint undertaking informed by the ideals and aspirations of a collective practice infused by value rationality and the commitment to valued social ends.
>
> (Fielding, 1999, p. 9)

Fielding's robust defence of the need to consider collegiality within any discussion of collaboration and collaborative cultures is in part a rebuttal of Hargreaves's (1994) scepticism about whether 'real' collaboration or collegiality actually existed within schools. Fielding argues for a radical or inclusive form of collegiality that recognises what is specific to education as a profession:

> First, and least contentiously of the three, there is the view that at the centre of a contemporary account of collegiality in education there lie dispositions and sought opportunities for teachers to learn with and from each other. Secondly, and more contentiously, there is the view that teaching is primarily a personal and not a technical activity and that at the heart of an educative encounter there is a mutuality of learning between the teacher and the student. On this view, students enter the collegium, not as objects of professional endeavour, but as partners in the learning process, and, on occasions, as teachers of teachers, not solely, or merely as perpetual learners. . . . Thirdly, and finally, there is a view that education in a democracy is necessarily characterised by a radical and universal inclusiveness which embraces, not just other teachers and not just one's students, but also parents and other members of the community in whose name the practice of education is both funded and intended. On this view, the collegium is further enlarged to include more fully and more energetically those who have for so long merited little more than contempt, indifference (cf. Burbules and Densmore, 1991) or the lip service of an unreal and unresolved partnership.
>
> (Fielding, 1999, p. 11)

For Fielding this latter form of collegiality is the only way within a democracy to ensure that schools and the education system as a whole function to achieve ethical social change and meet the needs of all those within it, rather than just those groups with the most power. His argument is that this form of radical collegiality is required if the end results we seek are truly 'educated' individuals, teachers and pupils, rather than simply more qualified pupils and more technically adept teachers.

By no means would all network leaders and members sign up to Fielding's inclusive view of collegiality but neither, in our experience, is their desire to work together generally driven by purely instrumental or short-term reasons. A view supported by our research, and others, that has highlighted how networks have opened up leadership opportunities and encouraged practitioners to learn from each other (Hadfield *et al.*, 2004a), has been influential in supporting the growth of students as researchers and student voice activities (McGregor and Fielding, 2005), and has had considerable successes in involving parents and local communities (Dyson, 2006). Our argument is that not only can we see echoes of Fielding's radical collegiality in action within many networks but also an implicit sense of this form of collegiality underpins the reasons why many practitioners engage in school networks. Our first answer to why should leaders and practitioners get involved in school networks is that in overtly competitive education systems, often bureaucratic school structures, and increasingly imposed curricula and pedagogies, they present an opportunity for practitioners to re-assert forms of collegiality that have been eroded.

If we turn from the micro- to the macro-political reasons why leaders and practitioners get involved in school networks then in the UK we would have to say that currently they are as likely to based on a desire to resist an external initiative or policy, overcome a lack of external support, or deal with the failure of a local or national policy as they are to be a positive assertion of new educational vision. It is perhaps telling that one of the first examples of collaboratives we researched was a political alliance between two secondary schools in a small town that was based on challenging the application to found a new selective school locally.

This situation perhaps reflects the 'tectonic drift' that underpins the current education landscape, at least in the UK, which is still drawing schools apart from other schools, and schools away from their communities. At the core of our education systems are the remnants of the old competitive policies and resulting naive managerialism that meant many leaders prioritised the educational attainment of 'their' school and 'their' pupils over the achievement of the pupils from 'our' community. Although pockets of schools working in networks are countering this drift, and in recent times there have been numerous policy initiatives encouraging school-to-school collaboration, the structural arrangements in many educational systems are far from being network based. They are still dominated by the single institution whose relationships with others are defined either by bureaucratic systems or free market economic models.

As we discuss in the final chapter of this book we believe that one possible future for school networks is that we will see their political actions moving on from being primarily about resisting external pressures to taking part in professional campaigns aimed at changing the debate as to what constitutes worthwhile education and fundamentally re-arranging the current educational landscape. Previously we have compared networks of schools to social movements (Hadfield, 2007), such as the ecology movement, because of the parallels between the leadership challenges faced by school leaders and campaign organisers in drawing together different groups to pursue a common purpose. We may in the future see even closer similarities.

We feel it is no coincidence that in the UK the increase in voluntary school networks has run in parallel with an increase in disaffection with a nationally imposed curriculum and the desire to develop local adaptations and inter-pretations. The second reason therefore that leaders and practitioners should get involved in school networks is that their ability to engage in concerted collective action gives them not only considerable campaigning ability but also the potential to fundamentally change the way in which the education system operates in a locality. Networks of schools are adopting new ways of dealing with school exclusions, community engagement and adapting curricula to meet local needs. These are developments that are slowly influencing notions of governance, who actually in a locality is, and should be, involved in decisions about the type of schools and the form of schooling that is provided. Being involved in a network can widen current leaders' sense of responsibility beyond their current school and 'their' pupils and engage them with issues of a different scale around the educational opportunities available to a whole community.

In summary, the political agendas that draw people into networks of schools can operate from the micro to the macro. At the micro level they are still inherently professional in that they hint at a form of collegiality that steps outside of the confines of practitioners' own schools and the short-term agendas of improving attainment. At the macro level they have only just started to raise questions about who determines the nature of the education provision on offer in a locality. They are still more often than not marked by a kind of 'resistance' culture based on the rejection of externally imposed policies and the idiosyncrasies of local politicians. Whether they will develop their own unique political identities is an issue we return to at the end of this book.

Chapter 2

Designing an effective school network

Introduction

If you are a school leader thinking about creating a new network, a researcher setting out to evaluate one, or a student interested in finding out more about their design then the plethora of different forms and types of networks makes each of these tasks seem equally daunting. In a review of different forms of network and learning communities, Kerr *et al.* (2003) identified nine core attributes of effective networks. Their analysis of the key features of effective school networks creates an important but challenging checklist for those designing, evaluating and monitoring a network of schools:

1   *Participation* – as we have already discussed networks are defined by the nature of their members' participation within it. The challenge for those who design networks is to combine and sustain the key forms of participation.
2   *Relationships and trust* – a common theme across the literature on networks, particularly in the early stages of design and implantation, is the importance of the 'soft' structures, such as trust, which bring people together.
3   *Coordination, facilitation and leadership* – networks need both vertical and horizontal forms of coordination, facilitation and leadership to keep people engaged and moving in a common direction.
4   *Communication* – communication is a process that needs both soft and hard structures to be in place.
5   *Structural balance* – network processes and structures need to be balanced. Too heavy a structure can drain initiative and strangle the dynamism of a network; too light a structure creates confusion and inhibits the growth of depth and reach in a network.
6   *Diversity and dynamism* – one of the powerful productive capacities of networks is they can bring together disparate people and ideas. It is often argued that volunteerism is an important part of ensuring the dynamic engagement of others.

7   *Decentralisation and democracy* – there are various types of network structures but all have a degree of decentralisation that allows participants to address local interests and issues while still operating within a collaborative environment that encourages inclusive and transparent decision making.

8   *Time and resources* – the research evidence is that network coordinators and facilitators are often overloaded and are constantly juggling competing priorities and demands. The network design needs to build in succession planning and try to prevent member burn-out.

9   *Monitoring and evaluation* – we discuss network evaluation as part of the broader issue of sustainability in Chapter 5. Processes though such as reflection and enquiry to highlight 'what works' and why are crucial within networks if they are not to dissipate their energies.

Although each of these characteristics needs to be borne in mind during the design process, our approach to this complex challenge is to suggest a simple design flow, one that starts with a consideration of the network's basic purposes, its aims and objectives, and flows through a consideration of agency and processes before eventually arriving at the point of designing its structures. We represent this 'flow' in Figure 2.1.

Once a network's overall purpose is clarified, consideration needs to be given to the forms of agency, both collective and individual, needed to achieve this. This assessment of a network's current capacity and its future needs should flow into a discussion of the kinds of processes required to build capacity in areas where it is low and that will allow existing capacity to be transferred around the network and harnessed to meet its aims. Finally, structures will be needed to manage and coordinate the processes that have been designed.

This flow was developed to avoid some of the classic limitations to network design we have come across in our own research. It is surprising the number of networks whose first decisions tend to be about structures, such as who will be on the strategic leadership group, or that continue to operate within structures originally designed for different purposes. This design flow is aimed at developing a network that is fit for purpose, and therefore hopefully both effective and efficient, which in turn makes it more likely to be sustainable.

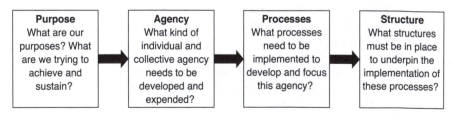

Purpose	**Agency**	**Processes**	**Structure**
What are our purposes? What are we trying to achieve and sustain?	What kind of individual and collective agency needs to be developed and expended?	What processes need to be implemented to develop and focus this agency?	What structures must be in place to underpin the implementation of these processes?

Figure 2.1 The design flow for a network

We now want to consider each phase of the design processes and discuss its connection with the other phases.

Purpose: developing a shared focus and the role of trust and mutual knowledge in allowing for informed challenges

In our design model the rest of the decisions flow once an agreed focus and shared vision have been established at least between the leaders of the network. (We provide an outline process for developing a focus at the end of the next chapter on establishing a network.) Selecting a shared focus that a substantial number of network members can buy into is not only important to building network identity, and hence helps support the development of a positive network culture (Hudson-Ross, 2001; Tell, 2000), but it is also key in terms of mobilising network resources. To do its job of engaging and mobilising staff the focus needs to fit within the scope of its members' professional practices, align with their professional values, and has to appear to be justifiable and worthwhile in terms of the expenditure of their limited resources.

Selecting a focus requires members of a network to engage critically and honestly with colleagues about what they want to achieve, and the values on which this decision is based, and it requires them to be open about the current issues and problems they face in their schools, as there is no point in setting unrealistic and unachievable aims. One of the major issues at this stage of the design process is how to ensure honest and open debate and addressing how, and if, individual schools can align their work accordingly. For example, at a practical level certain foci might mean schools having to change their development plans so that collaborative activity adds value to their improvement efforts. In the following quote a headteacher within a network points out that this process can be difficult even when a degree of trust already exists and may require the use of a facilitator, a role discussed in more detail in Chapter 6:

> The use of highly contextualised data to support the setting of a collaborative's strategic direction, identify current weaknesses and support change is critical. This requires a high degree of trust between those leading the network but it is also imperative that they do not slip into 'comfortable' collaboration. Support needs to be provided to leaders in challenging others and just as importantly how to receive and respond to these challenges. A facilitator of some form is often needed to establish these norms within a group of head teachers.
>
> (Headteacher quoted in Hadfield and Jopling, 2007)

Besides trust what is also needed is 'highly contextualised knowledge', particularly mutual knowledge not only of each other's schools but also about each other's approach to leadership, the challenges they face and their improvement efforts: 'We're working from the knowledge of each other and each other's schools . . .We know which schools are similar . . .We'll visit each other's schools to see how they are tackling issues' (Headteachers quoted in Hadfield and Jopling, 2007).

To extend Sachs's (2000, p. 82) evocative phrase, professional activism requires, 'not only that each party inhabit each other's castles, as Somekh (1994) suggest[s], but rather, that each party at least looks inside the other's castle'. An effective network design process requires not just looking inside each other's castles but also carrying out a structural survey of how they were built and where the weak spots are. This is because if networking is not to devolve into 'comfortable collaboration', trust and mutual knowledge needs to be supplemented by a willingness amongst leaders in a network to challenge each other. The 'warrant' of these challenges is that in closely knit networks they are made by leaders working in the same dynamic and complex situations and have the credibility of working with the 'same kind of pupils and staff'. The competence and expertise of those making these challenges will be judged in these arenas on criteria set by their peers, not by external inspection regimes or other external agencies.

Generating informed and credible challenges is a particularly significant issue for those designing networks of schools operating in inner cities and other complex and challenging contexts. Here a great deal of external pressure to improve usually already exists but is more often than not based on 'official' data and not on the basis of mutual knowledge. This means that challenges when made are often perceived as coming from an 'outsider' perspective rather than from someone who understands the 'realities' of the situation. Leaders in such situations can become defensive and dismissive of the achievements of other similar schools, and so reinforce a culture of low expectations, simply because they do not know these schools and their leaders well enough. If though a higher achieving school in the same network is used as a comparison school and the leaders of this school are making the challenges then they are much more difficult to dismiss. Those developing networks in any circumstances will have to deal sensitively with leaders' resistance to being challenged and dismissive attitudes based on a lack of understanding. To do this they need to build up sufficient trust and mutual knowledge between leaders so that they will feel comfortable being challenged and challenging others. If insufficient trust exists at the beginning of the design process this needs to be dealt with. Getting in an external facilitator, who is respected by all the leaders of a network, to identify the issues in each school and facilitate a process where these are shared is a good starting point while the longer term process of trust building takes place.

Defining the purpose of a network needs to take place in a context of mutual trust and informed challenge in order not only to keep leaders 'honest' about their work and the achievements of their school, but also for the next stage of the design process to be successful. This is where leaders have to be realistic about the current capacities within their schools and how they will be used to meet the network's aims.

Networked agency: what is best done together and what is best done alone?

During this design phase the first question that network leaders have to ask themselves is: What scale of collective action do you imagine your staff and school being involved in to achieve the network aims the network has set?

Expectations about working collaboratively can vary enormously. On the one hand, some leaders may simply wish their staff to learn from staff in other schools, while others will want much more collective action. This may just be a case of joining up subject specialists across schools to change what is happening in key departments or the formation of specialised cross-school teams to deliver a new initiative in the local community. But on the other hand, the network's aims might be seen as requiring all staff to work on an aspect of whole-school change. Getting clarity of how the network will operate is based on being clear about the extent to which different leaders see this as simply collaborative professional development or as an opportunity for staff to work collectively between and within each other's schools. This is important because many school leaders, particularly at the start of a network, can be nervous about 'losing' control and having other staff working in their school.

The term networked agency describes the balance between collaborative learning and collective action within a network. The balance in a network will depend not only upon its purposes but also how comfortable its leaders are with the idea of collective action. In some professional networks the vast majority of members do not act collectively at all, they will simply attend joint professional development activities. In these networks the individual draws upon the expertise in the network to inform their practice but does not work collectively towards achieving a shared agenda for change. Many national subject specialist networks have this balance of collaborative learning and collective agency. In contrast other networks set out to explicitly invoke collective action at levels ranging from individual departments to whole schools, and in some cases they aspire to affect educational provision across a whole locality. One such network-based initiative was the Networked Learning Communities (NLC) programme (Jackson and Payne, 2003) in the UK, which set out to develop a form of collective agency that '[e]ncompasses the notion of building capacity within schools and networks so that they promote not just school or network level learning but system wide learning' (Jackson, 2005, p. 8).

The NLC programme aimed to promote collective action not only between schools but also between networks so that their collective actions might radically change what was on offer to local communities. To achieve this level of collective action they needed to develop the capacities of individuals, schools and whole networks to learn and work together. They called the process of capacity building 'networked learning':

> Networked learning is at the heart of collaborative capacity building. It occurs where people from different schools in a network engage with one another to enquire into practice, to innovate, to exchange knowledge and to learn together. Unlike 'networking', perhaps, it doesn't happen by accident and, in order to happen by design, alternative organisational patterns, new professional relationships and different forms of facilitation, intervention and brokerage are required.
>
> (Jackson, 2005, p. 12)

Once they have decided upon the balance between collaborative learning and collective action, what network leaders have to ask themselves is whether they already have the individual and collective capacity they need to meet the purposes and aims they have set out for the network. Assessing individual capacities is relatively familiar ground for most leaders as they often have to consider if staff have the skills, knowledge and dispositions to engage in a range of professional practices and implement new ideas and policies. A more unfamiliar challenge is assessing what Sullivan and Skelcher (2003) termed the 'capacity for collaboration'. They created this term to highlight the issue that developing collective agency, the ability to achieve change through working together, is not simply a matter of collecting together all the little bits of individual agency that exist. Rather, getting individuals to work collectively towards a shared aim requires specific skills and understandings such as, as we discuss in more detail in Chapter 3, the political skills of mobilisation and the cultural skills of coherence making, and these can defeat even the most skilful institutional leader.

Once the degree of collective action required is clarified, and the extent to which the capacity for this exists already, then the network leader has only two more design decisions to make. How are they going to harness what already exists? How are they going to develop any capacity, individual or collective, that is lacking in the network? These two questions should lead the designers of the network on to the next stage, that of designing the key processes that need to be put in place to both harness and develop individual and collective agency across the network.

Processes: coordination and generation

Put simplistically there are two main types of processes in every network that are productive of both individual and collective capacity and both need to be considered at the design phase. There are the coordination processes needed to harness current capacity within the network and the generative processes that develop those that are absent or in short supply. These two sets of processes need to be designed so that they interact effectively. When this happens, harnessing the current capacity of people to work together will, because the experience is positive, produce further capacity. In addition the early generative processes will have processes built into them that will support their coordination so as the network develops it does not become overburdened by a management structure or stultified by a 'meetings' culture. So, for example, a CPD process that sets out to develop certain new skills and knowledge also needs a process built into it that will coordinate and link existing and new capacities. This may seem a little 'chicken and egg' but a key to early success is that the major processes that a network invests in do 'double-duty' in that they both develop and coordinate capacity.

The nature of these early interactions, and how they develop, is highly dependent on the origins of a network. Some groups of schools volunteer to work together, others do so because incentives are available, while some are subjected to external pressure. The fact that networks come together for different purposes, and start at various points, means their members can have very different intentions and aspirations for their participation, and this will affect the scope and intensity of these initial processes.

There is though an emerging, if somewhat limited, consensus as to the kinds of processes that are key in the initial stages of network formation. After carrying out a meta-analysis of 17 school networks, based on case reports produced by four different research teams, Hadfield and Jopling (2007) concluded that effective networks in their initial stages focused on a limited number of processes:

- articulating shared values and a common focus;
- building trust and mutual knowledge;
- developing a strategic approach to continuing professional development.

As we have already discussed the need to articulate a common focus in the previous section, we will focus now on the latter two processes.

Designing in trust building processes

Trust, cooperation, lack of competitiveness between the schools and their staff is cited again and again as the foundation for the current work . . . This trust is the outcome of many years of working together and of a conscious attitude towards working on the part of the Head Teachers involved. The trust has been built up around a shared vision. This vision is one of coherent and holistic education for children: that children's education takes place here not just within individual schools.

(Headteacher quoted in Hadfield and Jopling, 2007)

The concept of trust is not only a foundation of the above headteacher's network but also is seen as a basis for collaboration and networking throughout the literature (Branch *et al.*, 1995; Berliner, 1997; Newell and Swan, 2000; Skidmore, 2004; Day and Hadfield, 2004; Ainscow *et al.*, 2006). Trust is seen as playing a vital role in everything from collaboration within political and community activism, in for example Giddens (1994), to models of educational change (Hargreaves and Fullan, 1992). More recently as social network theory has been applied to the study of businesses and markets there has been a massive expansion in the literature around networks and trust, particularly as the idea of greater networking and increased social capital has been shown to provide a competitive advantage to individuals and companies (Burke, 2005). Trust is often termed the 'glue' that holds together networks, but what kind of glue is it and what processes are needed to develop it?

> Trust is a willingness to commit to a collaborative effort before you know how the person will behave. Distrust is a reluctance to commit without guarantees about the other person's behaviour. This is trust pure and simple. You anticipate cooperation from the other person, but you commit to the exchange before you know how the other person will behave.
>
> (Burt, 2001, p. 3)

Trust between members of a network is so important because it glues together a mass of individual agency so it can become collective action targeted at achieving a shared aim. Trust between network members is so important that when designing a network processes need to be put in place that protect, nurture and develop it.

To do this we need to think how trust originates and develops in various types of relationships and through different processes. Newell and Swan (2000) in their study of networking relationships between research institutions make a distinction between three sources of trust. First, companion trust is that which exists amongst friends and is based within their friendships. The kinds of processes that develop this are essentially social in nature. One therefore should not underestimate the social dimension to network processes and build in time for this by considering how people can network informally in a meeting to developing more 'formalised' social events. Second, competence trust exists amongst colleagues who know that they will complete an agreed task. This is the 'quick win' phenomenon, where early success breeds further collaboration. Opportunities for such quick wins need to be built into the early stages of network processes. Third, contractual trust is based on a belief that sufficiently strong legal or institutional arrangements are in place to ensure that what is agreed takes place. Although legal contracts are rare, many networks have agreed structures and processes based on collective responsibility. For example, we have seen networks where each organisation has raised a levy based on the number of pupils in each school. The funds generated were then allocated on the basis of collective decision making. If a school failed to participate in the decision making processes they would not be allocated funding. Once allocated, network members monitored each other's use of funds and these would be returned if there was insufficient take up within an individual school or collaborative project. These strong institutional arrangements helped develop the level of trust in the network to the point that allowed them to share their scarce resources.

In the early stages of a school network trust will probably arise from a mixture of companion and competence-based trust with contractual trust being of very little relevance. If though the collaboration deepens and extends to more formalised, and possibly expensive, collaborative projects then trust based in mutual competence and more explicit arrangements will become dominant. This shift is illustrated in the quote used at the beginning of this section. It is quite common to find the origins of school networks amongst groups of headteachers and principals who operate in the same locality and initially may have come together through attending the same events and meetings. They then build up an informal support system, based on companion trust, which then progresses to some form of joint working, which if it is successful will give rise to competence-based trust. What is often forgotten, or overlooked, by these leaders is the need for similar sorts of trust to be developed at all levels of the network. Particularly as other network participants may not have had the luxury of developing trust more naturally over time so its cultivation needs to be designed into the early processes within the network.

As people begin to work together more frequently and to develop mutual knowledge of each other then a final form of trust develops, this is identification-based trust (Sheppard and Tuchinsky, 1996; Church et al., 2002). This kind of trust was initially identified in the study of networks within political movements and showed how a common ideological position, with its mixture of shared analyses and collective sense of what needed to be done, created a strong bond of trust between those in such movements. The processes of building this kind of trust should start at the initial stages of designing a network by selecting a focus that allows those in the networks to articulate and recognise their shared values where they exist and to come to agreement around what are the common challenges they face and what should be their collective response. From this basis this form of trust should emerge out of sustained collective action where it is particularly important because it supports autonomy and flexibility: 'Identity-based trust makes it possible for a person, group or firm to permit a partner to act independently – knowing its interests will get met' (Sheppard and Tuchinsky, 1996, p. 145).

The strength of the 'glue' provided by the identification-based trust is dependent on the nature of the network focus and the degree of collective action it requires. If the focus requires no more that a broad commitment to 'putting children first' or 'teaching and learning' then agreeing to this is unlikely to be problem amongst the majority of network members, but neither will it be a strong bond. If though the focus is based on more specific values, for example commitment to a specific pedagogy or resistance to an imposed external agenda, and it requires sustained collective action across the network, then it may be more problematic to agree in the short term but will create a much stronger bond in the longer term.

Trust, its nurture and management, lies at the heart of one of the major design tensions within building a network. On the one hand if we want to maximise trust in a network we limit our 'relational risk' (Nooteboom, 2007) and work only with those we know already. That is we design our network around existing close relationships, in which people know one another, where there is an established degree of reciprocity, and where if things go wrong sanctions can be enforced. On the other hand to make the most of networks and the costs involved with them they need to be designed so they bridge the 'holes' in our established professional networks. These holes are the gaps in our existing networks that mean we lack awareness of new innovations and practices or the support to tackle a current problem. The tension arises in that trying to bridge these gaps will mean working with people and institutions with whom you do not have a strong relationship and this presents a higher degree of risk taking. This balance between being risk averse and maximising the potential benefits of collaboration runs through the literature on networking.

The strategic development of effective collaborative professional development

Our research showed that developing trust was one of the basic 'social' processes that underpinned the initial development of networks. It is the glue that sticks together existing capacity so that it could be made to work collectively. The next key process that networks developed was some form of learning process capable of generating further capacity. Getting network members to learn from, and with, one another lies at the heart of most school networks. The development of collaborative professional development opportunities at all levels within schools, from leaders through pupils to parents, appeared to be the key to successful network initiation, and sustainability as we discuss in the following chapters. Any old learning process will not do and our research and that of others (Hadfield et al., 2005) is full of examples of launch conferences that didn't lead to sustained networking and poorly facilitated action research groups that affected no substantive change in the classroom. At the point of designing a network its leaders need to create opportunities for strategic thinking and planning about the types of learning relationships they wish to develop.

One of the headteachers in Hadfield and Jopling's (2007) research reflected on the role of a critical group of peers drawn from across other schools in the network in stimulating their own thinking about the nature of learning and in doing so helped move the school on from the comfortable 'plateau' it had occupied for some years:

> I think our school after I'd been here about six or seven years was at a plateau. And I think it, the network, allowed us to take off again. I've

never felt at a plateau since . . .. I think we'd got the quality of teaching
to as effective a level as we could and I couldn't see where to go next. . . .
And because of working in a network of schools, where there needs to be
vision and direction – this direction and vision was very clearly centred
around learning, improving the quality of learning, improving opportunities for learning, improving our learning and our understanding of
that learning, and learning at pupil, staff, head level. It suddenly opened
things up for me. Far from being at the top of a plateau looking down, I
feel that I'm at the bottom of a mountain looking up.

> (Headteacher quoted in Hadfield and Jopling, 2007, p. 7)

Generating this sense of professional renewal and a revived interest in their
own learning is a common theme amongst leaders of effective school networks.
Planning strategically for the development of a network requires leaders to
move on from engaged and fundamental discussions about the nature of
learning to a consideration of how to operationalise powerful learning processes
across a network.

Designing the processes needed to develop a wider range of capacities across
a network is both technically and culturally difficult as it requires the leaders
to answer a range of questions about what kinds of capacities are to be built
and where. Which capacities are key? Do we need to build these in any
particular order? Are we going to build them at the level of key individuals,
school-based teams, whole schools or in cross-school groups? Do we have the
leadership capacity to even start this process or do we need to build that
first?

Being strategic means taking into consideration a range of factors so it is
difficult to offer specific advice, but in the initial stages of a network leaders
often decide initially to build the required capacities within small groups of
individuals who are then given within-school and across-school responsibilities
for developing its further development. In our own research (Hadfield et al.,
2004b) we have described the early development of two networks that provide
an example of this flow from the identification of network foci through to the
development of a series of learning processes focused on a specific group of
individuals who then worked in cross-school groups to impact on schools.

Vignette: the Hartlepool network (adapted from Hadfield et al., 2004a)

The Hartlepool network was made up of 12 primaries and one special school
and was based in the medium-sized town of Hartlepool: a compact town of
just under 100,000 people in which there were significant pockets of
unemployment. The steering group of mainly headteachers decided to hire an
external consultant to advise them at a strategic level and to carry out practical
tasks to ensure the network kept moving along.

The consultant's first task was to interview each of the headteachers to identify what they felt were the 'barriers to learning' in their schools. The outcome of this was a paper prepared for the steering group in which he outlined what the schools hoped to get out of being part of the network, what specific areas the headteachers felt the network should address, what the key professional development issues were in their schools and what concerns they had about participating in the network.

This data was then used to identify nine key issues that research groups might be interested in enquiring about. A 'declaration form' was then created for distribution to schools inviting each school to nominate three teachers to become part of one of the research groups. As well as asking for an area of interest the declaration form also asked teachers to indicate whether they wished to be part of a research group, a study group or a coaching partnership.

Some of the headteachers presented this form to their whole staff and where schools found they had more than three volunteers then these were accommodated. In other schools the headteachers had been keen to ensure that if this key activity was to be successful it needed to involve the right people so they were more selective in seeking out volunteers. In the end 42 teachers volunteered to be part of the enquiry groups. The headteachers felt that they could have had many research groups but had concerns about sustaining the scale of anything bigger and of spreading their financial resources too thinly. There was a real sense in the headteacher group that making a success of this was fundamental to the future success of the network.

The consultant gathered together the declaration forms and from these returns formed the volunteer teachers into nine research groups or coaching partnerships, each one addressing an area of interest in a forum of choice and a mix of teachers from different schools in each.

The Hartlepool network therefore aligned its learning processes very clearly with its network focus of removing the barriers to learning its pupils faced. The nine practitioner research groups each targeted an issue that had been identified by the headteacher group. In the end this group of headteachers went on to develop their own learning processes as they enquired into the work of the research groups and as they took on the role of facilitators to these groups.

The above vignette is an example of a learning process that was both generative of new capacity and brought together what it generated with existing capacity. To underpin these generative and coordinating processes the Hartlepool network had to develop a series of structures or a network infrastructure to monitor and support the work of the research groups.

Network structures: underpinning the processes

As we have already discussed a structure, in networks terms, is any means of bringing people together. What is meant by 'bringing together' in a 'networked society' (Castells, 2001, p. 1) in which networks, 'are very old forms of human practice but have taken on a new life in our time by becoming information networks' is changing rapidly. This is especially the case when communication can be carried out over huge distances by email and videophones and where individuals can 'gather' synchronously and asynchronously on the internet. There is little common agreement on what works in terms of network structures (Kerr *et al.*, 2003) which can guide a designer. Instead structures tend to be discussed as a series of trade-offs between, for example, structures that are formal top-down control mechanisms with those that are more informal, supportive and bottom-up (Lieberman, 1996, 1999).

Although network structures can be consciously and externally designed they will inevitably reflect the influence of what we might term internal 'drivers' that also shape them. The first of these is the presence within the network of 'organisers'; these are key people, groups or schools that serve as a 'hub'. These organisers sit at the centre of a great deal of activity and due to their interest, capacity or power they orchestrate the work of other members of the network. A second driver is the pattern of prior connections in a network. This patina of pre-existing connections can be particularly influential in the early stages of network development and will re-emerge throughout the life of a network. Finally, the nature and scope of the joint work being undertaken will eventually create its own structures that arise out of the needs and communication patterns between the individuals and small groups of teachers involved, rather than be imposed by any network leaders. When designing a network structure it is important that the current and potential influences of these drivers are recognised and built into the plan for how the infrastructure will develop.

There are a number of classical 'designs' used to categorise different network infrastructures, see Starkey (1997). These designs represent both the conscious decisions of network leaders and reflect the influence of the patina of previous connections and existing power relationships within the network.

A simple but very common structure for a network of schools is a 'hub and spoke' model (as shown in Figure 2.2).

At the centre of this network is a central powerful organiser through which flows the vast majority of network activity. It draws in the other organisations and coordinates their work within the network, although there are always a certain amount of connections that do not go through it. The kinds of networks that have these kinds of infrastructures are the simpler university–school networks. For example the 'Improving the Quality of Education for All' (IQEA) school improvement programme in the United Kingdom (Hopkins and Lagerweij, 1996), although it has evolved over time and taken on a number of forms, has in its long history been run out of a number of universities that have acted as its hub. The IQEA improvement programme, or reform package, was developed to be delivered to groups of schools by university staff. Its long-term

Figure 2.2
A hub and spoke network

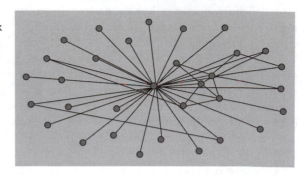

sustainability though was premised on increasingly bringing in school-based staff who had developed expertise either in enquiry-based approaches to whole-school reform or a specific pedagogical or curriculum innovation. Certain schools might then develop sufficient capacity to become hubs in their own right. This could lead to an IQEA network of schools developing into next classic example of a school network, a 'hub and nodes' structure.

A hub and nodes network is one in which there is still a single central organisational focus but it only links directly to a number of 'node' points, not directly to all the members of the network. These node organisations act as mini-hubs and orchestrate the majority of network activity (see Figure 2.3).

Each of these mini-hubs might adopt different foci for their 'own' clusters and a very different approach to networking. Such networks might develop from the centre outwards, as was the case with the IQEA programme, where a central organisation, a university, spawned a number of mini-networks across the UK. The alternative is that the mini-networks pre-exist prior to their connection by a central organisation. For example, Ruddock discusses how a team of university researchers helped a local authority bring together three beacon schools clusters, similar to lighthouse schools in the US and navigator schools in Australia. As each cluster consisted of a beacon school and two or three other schools, a network of some 11 schools was formed. Interestingly the aim of this network was to 'unlock the expertise and insight of teachers in the host or beacon schools' (Ruddock *et al.*, 2000, p. 266). Thus the flow of this network was very much 'in' from its peripheries to the centre where this expertise would then be redistributed around the rest of the network. A somewhat different flow existed in the more centralised IQEA networks, which tended to flow from the centre outwards.

DECENTRALISED
(B)

Figure 2.3 A nodal network

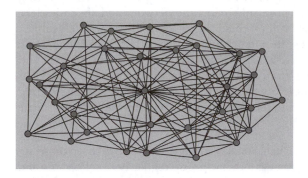

Figure 2.4
A crystalline network

The final classic organisational infrastructure is the 'crystalline' structure. To an extent this kind of structure reflects an 'idealised' rather than a practical working image of a real network. These kinds of networks are not only very tightly knitted but there is a symmetry to their interconnections, to the extent that there appears to be no one coordinating hub and each member of the network acts as a cross linked node (see Figure 2.4).

As an idealised image it is not surprising that it is difficult to identify practical examples of this kind of network in the field of education in the UK, at least not ones that have been sustained at the level of school-to-school networks. This is not to say that there are not examples of networks of schools that have attempted to achieve this level of connectedness and symmetry in their networking. Within the Network Learning Programme (Jackson and Payne, 2003), some of the 126 networks involved aspired to develop such highly integrated approaches, amongst them the WACO network of six secondary schools.

Vignette: WACO, an 'almost' crystalline network

This collaborative was based on six secondary schools that had initially been grouped together under the auspices of the Department for Education and Skills (DfES) who had brought in the IQEA team to support them as a network. Being part of the IQEA programme had given them the experience of working within a classical university–school network based around a simple hub and spoke structure. When they applied to become part of the NLC programme the IQEA programme had finished and they aspired to become a different form of network and to move on from collaborative learning to collective action:

> Rather than just sharing, we developed a model where we could work together, where teachers could work together, where teachers from each of the schools could come together and truly collaborate on the development of themes which were pertinent to all of the schools.
>
> (Network co-leader)

The network was steered by a research and development group consisting of the headteachers from each school within the network and six co-leaders. The network was effectively run by these six co-leaders, who were all subject leaders or middle managers in one of the six schools. Each co-leader ran a network theme group that drew its membership from across the network and recruited 'theme champions' from each school. The co-leaders framed the focus for the theme group and developed expertise in the themes through 'reading and web based research', while the theme champions led the cadre or theme groups based in each school.

> We've got our Theme Champions within schools for each of those six themes. They meet together as a theme group regularly to collaborate and develop the ideas which they then bring back into school and feed back into the normal working of the school. Each group is charged with coming up with a package really, that could be used in each of the schools to develop teaching and learning with the key aim of influencing what's going on in the classroom and enhancing the quality of learning.
>
> (Network co-leader)

Although WACO's own organ-o-gram (see Figure 2.5) represented their network as hierarchical the degree of interaction between the co-leaders, theme groups and school cadre groups' account meant that in actuality each school acted as a node to departments and groups in each of the five other schools. They were able to do this because themes were relevant to each school in the network and during their time within the NLC programme these themes were:

- student data and feedback to promote learning;
- expanding the teaching and learning repertoire;
- assessment for learning;
- the use of information and communication technologies;
- strategies for transition from Key Stages 2–3;
- independent learning.

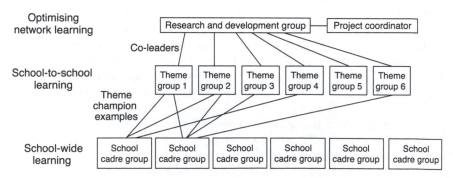

Figure 2.5 An organ-o-gram

Although the network was trying to develop these simultaneously in each school, there was recognition that even if equal collaborative equal effort was put into each theme there was likely to be differential take-up within each school:

> We did discuss if we could bring the themes on line in a sequence according to priorities and some schools would dip in and out according to their individual priorities. In the end, we decided to run all six themes together, but in effect, I think the success of those themes within individual schools does depend on the school's priorities.
>
> (Assistant headteacher)

In each theme there would be a 'lead' school and a collection of 'lead' departments, which had the responsibility of ensuring change occurred at the classroom level and disseminating and supporting the transfer of good practice within and across schools. This meant that unlike node and hubs design not only was there a comparatively equal flow of interactions but also at different times within the themes, schools and departments would move from being leaders to followers and vice versa. Such an elaborate and highly connected networking as exhibited by WACO is difficult to sustain without a considerable call on external funding, and in this instance had arisen over several years and was therefore based on deep patina of interactions, both professional and personal, that had built up over these years.

When thinking about network structures it would be a gross over-simplification to talk of them going through a developmental sequence from hub and spoke, through nodes and finally to a more crystalline structure. This would suggest that one form was essentially more effective or efficient than another, an issue that cannot be determined separately from discussing their aims and composition. There is though a case to be made that certain network structures are potentially more robust and therefore more sustainable than others. A more robust network structure would have the following features:

- greater redundancy;
- greater symmetry;
- greater reciprocity.

Greater redundancy means there are multiple connections between organisations, so a network is more likely to survive the loss of an individual member or be less affected by it. For example, if a node school were to leave a network then the whole mini-network it supported could also be lost as these schools lose their contact point to the larger network. If though there were alternative 'redundant' connections than those that ran through the node school, then these could be activated to reconnect it to the rest of the network.

Similarly in networks where there is a greater symmetry within the structure so individual schools can operate both as leaders and followers, senders and receivers, hubs and spokes, there is much greater likelihood that schools will maintain their commitment to the network. This is not just because schools can draw on and mobilise capacity from a broader range of other schools. It also means that an individual school's involvement in a network is never simply a question of being a 'cost', because they are always acting as a lead school or providing external capacity for other schools. Conversely, neither are they always being constructed as deficient in some way and so requiring support. If the structure of a network supports reciprocal working then schools can more effectively match their engagement to their own stage of development and internal capacity. Research into networked social movements (Oberschall, 1973) has also shown that in networks with more closely knitted structures it is easier to mobilise resources and avoid 'free-riding'. The shorter the linkages between organisations, and the fewer steps between them, the easier it is to lever in their support to the network.

The overall design flow was created to support those launching a network in moving from a consideration of their collective purpose through to designing its structure (see Table 2.1). It was a flow created in part to prevent some of the worse excesses of the network leaders and funders we have encountered in our research and development work who had become overly concerned with structures. As we discuss later on in the book the nature of networks mean that their leaders will need to keep revisiting their purpose and in doing so turn this linear flow into a series of design cycles as their network matures and evolves.

Tool 2.1: what kind of network suits your kind of school?

This tool is based on the idea that different types of schools are best suited to different types of networks and networking. It basically asks you to place your school into one of four categories:

- high capacity;
- medium capacity;
- low capacity;
- negative capacity.

Then it consider the nature of the networking that can help your school develop and the types of network activities that are most likely to support your school, and that your school could offer to the network.

This tool can also be used collectively by groups of leaders thinking of forming a network as it allows them to consider the nature of the schools within the network and the overall balance of capacity between them.

Table 2.1 Advice for network leaders on designing a network

Purpose	Defining the purpose of a network needs to take place in a context of mutual trust and informed challenge. If your focus requires no more than a broad set of commitment and collaborative learning then this it is unlikely to be problematic but neither will it be a strong bond. If it is based on more specific values and collective action it will be more difficult to get agreement but it will also create a much stronger bond.
Network agency	What is best done together and what is best done alone? What balance do you want between collaborative learning and collective action? Do you have the collaborative capacity needed to work together?
Processes	Trust between network members is so important that when designing a network processes need to be put in place that protect, nurture and develop it. Which capacities are key to achieving your aims? Do you need to build these in any particular order? Are you going to build them at the level of key individuals, schools-based teams, whole schools or in cross-school groups? Do you have the leadership capacity to even start this process or do we need to build that first? How are you going to develop any capacities that are lacking in the network?
Structure	Structures tend to be a series of trade-offs between being formal top-down control mechanisms with those that are more informal, supportive and bottom-up. The design of network structures needs to reflect the influence of internal 'drivers' such as the presence of powerful organisers, the patina of existing relationships and the growth of new structures out of interactions. How robust is your network in terms of redundancy, symmetry and reciprocity?

Assessing the current level of your school's capacity

Photocopy pages 42–43 and fold back the final column so it is underneath the sheet and cannot be seen by those completing the task. Get them to read through the following statements and tick the *eight* they see as most closely reflecting the current situation with their schools. Once they have gone through the list, get them to fold out the final column and total up the score.

Below 10 = Negative capacity
10–15 = Low capacity
15–20 = Medium capacity
20+ = High capacity

My school	Tick the box	Score
Our overall knowledge and skills base is poor and teachers have access to few CPD opportunities.	☐	1
It's fair to say our knowledge and skills base is low.	☐	2
CPD is viewed as key and individuals are encouraged to explore their own interests and needs beyond those found in the school development plan.	☐	4
Pupils, parents and the wider community are involved with many aspects of school life.	☐	4
We have a newly appointed headteacher.	☐	2
The school has developed strong networks with other educational organisations and the wider community.	☐	4
The senior leadership team promote a very distributed form of leadership that provides opportunities for all to develop their leadership skills.	☐	4
There are focused attempts to improvement learning and teaching and some good structures are in place.	☐	3
Variations in working practices are large and policies are not adhered to consistently.	☐	1
The management team has recently created new structures for the school.	☐	2
The structures in place to support pupils are inefficient and ineffective.	☐	1
Our teachers mostly work under close and prescriptive supervision from the management team.	☐	2
Teachers regularly working together within departments or phases and sometimes across them.	☐	3
We have well-established links with the community.	☐	3
We need to raise CPD, but have still to make significant inroads into doing this.	☐	2
Relationships within the school between teachers are quite fractured.	☐	1
The senior leadership team has delegated many leadership responsibilities to middle managers.	☐	3

Statement		Value
At the moment most leadership in the school is top down.	☐	2
Professional development needs of individuals are starting to be met and CPD opportunities are increasing within the school.	☐	3
I think we tend to exist in a state of continual minor crises.	☐	1
Individual teachers regularly discuss pupils' performance with them and with their colleagues.	☐	4
We have an interim management team.	☐	2
Teachers mostly rely on their own strengths or work within small cliques.	☐	1
There is a clear plan for improving the whole school.	☐	3
There are mechanisms in place to ensure and maintain teaching quality and accountability.	☐	3
The teacher culture in the schools is highly collaborative with teachers regularly working with each other and those from other schools.	☐	4
We have few formal monitoring/accountability systems because staff are highly trusted and self-critical.	☐	4
Data are considered to be important and are used regularly to inform decision making.	☐	3
We are making efforts to improve relations with the local community and the media.	☐	2
We rarely systematically use data to inform what we do.	☐	1
The senior leadership team is keen to disperse leadership to middle managers.	☐	3
Teachers have significant responsibility for day-to-day and strategic decision making.	☐	4

Negative capacity (below 10)

Our experience would suggest that in their current state most schools in this category are unsuitable for participation in a network unless it is well established and has the capacity to work with them. This is because schools in this category are likely to lack the structures and leadership to allow them to engage effectively with a network and learn from and with it. It may be possible to create a reserve of external capacity for such schools to draw down but because of the somewhat chaotic way in which they operate this will soon dissipate without any real impact.

Low capacity (10–15)

Schools in this category are likely to benefit from tightly directed networks that have established programmes that provide examples of good practice and models of teaching and learning. For these schools, especially in the early stages, it is important that there is a teaching and learning content within the programme. However, as confidence and skills develop within a network, the content-driven element is likely to become less important. This will facilitate a gradual shift from more directed activities to a more organic approach.

Medium capacity (15–20)

These schools have the most to gain from entering into a network that contains processes that set out to affect learning at different levels from leaders to pupils and parents. They will be able to cope with dispersed leadership across the network and to take on the more challenging learning processes such as enquiry and action research. The network will have to support senior leaders in devolving power and decision making processes further and in encouraging middle-level leaders and classroom teachers to take on such roles and responsibilities.

High capacity (20+)

These schools are already likely to be involved in a wide range of formal and informal networks and have accrued considerable experience. If this is the case then the challenge here is to extend the quality and quantity of activity beyond what has previously been thought possible within the organisation and to feed the expertise back into the system at another level. These schools therefore might wish to become a hub within a network, which would allow them to feed back their innovations to other schools. They might though wish to take on more radical forms of collaboration and networking.

Chapter 3

Establishing a school-based network

Introduction

In the previous chapter we set out the major issues that need to be considered when designing a network. Now we move on to providing advice and insights into how to get things started in the early phases of establishing a network. This chapter sets out to answer questions such as:

- How do you go about developing a focus?
- How do you mobilise people at different layers of the network so that they work together collaboratively?
- What does it take to get people to identify with and feel they own the network they are part of?
- If trust is so important, how do you develop it?

We answer these questions by providing you with insights from existing network leaders, by sharing with you some of the tools we have developed to support networks, and by again providing you with short case studies of networks we have come across in our own research.

Where to start?

How you go about establishing your network depends on your starting position. Some networks are put together by external agencies as they try and improve schooling in an area. Other networks come about as groups of senior leaders from different schools meet and discuss their individual schools and find they are either facing similar problems or share common interests and aspirations. Others may arise from a shared sense of isolation or in response to external funding opportunities. Each of these various starting points requires a different approach not only because they aspire to different ends but also because they emerge from different beginnings.

In this chapter we are going to discuss possibly the most common scenario and one that certainly has general relevance as it encapsulates the main stages and issues in establishing a network. In this scenario a group of leaders from across several schools in a locality, some of whom know each other already, begin to meet repeatedly as a result of being involved in support programme provided by their local authority or school district. At some point in this programme those senior leaders who already know each other well, because they have worked in the area for some time or previously worked in each other's schools, begin to develop an idea of working more collaboratively and a number of cross-school projects are suggested. These projects begin to attract the attention of the other leaders on the programme and fairly soon the notion of creating a network emerges. A sub-group of the more enthusiastic leaders begins to formalise a network proposal and comes up with a basic plan.

In this scenario, in common with many others, the first stages in establishing a network is to move the idea for the network out from a group of activists, who know each other well, to a wider group of leaders and then eventually to all those who will eventually become involved in the network. Stott (Stott *et al.*, 2006) in her discussion of network building makes a crucial distinction between the motivations of these activists, and the processes they use to develop the initial idea, and how to motivate others, and the processes needed to do this.

The initial group of activists have had a chance to discuss their motivations and to define the shared purposes for the network. However the network leaders need to make a clear distinction between the motivations and purposes of these early activists, whom Stott describes as a 'seed', and the establishment of an overarching purpose for the larger network so that it becomes a network of schools rather than simply a group of individuals (see Figure 3.1).

One of the most common mistakes in the early life of a network occurs when the activists fail to recognise that they need to use different approaches for drawing in other leaders who have to this point been less involved and when bringing their staff on board. What results if they don't is a small group of activists who quickly become a clique rather than a network:

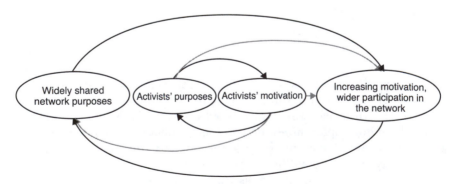

Figure 3.1 Moving from a group of individuals to a network of schools

The big danger . . . is that they could have a relatively small number of highly committed and enthusiastic learners sharing their learning with each other across the network without drilling down and spreading widely within their individual schools . . . it's easier to work in an innovative way with people who are as excited by it and enthusiastic about it as you are.

(Network facilitator)

The first key point then in establishing a network is to make a clear distinction between the processes used in working with enthusiasts and those used to bring in other key leaders and the mass of practitioners, a distinction we have termed micro and macro mobilisation.

This distinction is based on our research, Hadfield *et al.* (2005), where we broke the process of mobilising and motivating others to become involved not only into two main stages, micro and macro mobilisation, but also showed how it was based on four key leadership activities: courting, aligning, connecting and embedding (see Table 3.1).

Table 3.1 The leadership of mobilisation

		Leadership activity	Example
Micro mobilisation	Courting	Approaching potential partners, developing proposals for new networked activity.	• Collecting contacts and courting possible networked partnerships. • Building links with leaders with similar foci or those who offer learning opportunities.
	Aligning	Winning leadership buy-in through individual or group negotiation. Preparing plans for the network that reflect their areas of concern.	• Developing mission statements, network-wide focus or specific enquiry foci. • Whole-school target-setting and strategy building. • Establishing of steering groups.
Macro mobilisation	Connecting	Creating structured opportunities for teachers to work together.	• Establishing and allocating network-based roles and responsibilities. • Skill development to lead, facilitate or participate in networks such as leadership training or presentation skills.
	Embedding	Institutionalising the network through its formal links within and between schools and growth of informal relationships.	• Creation of lead learner forums, cadre groups, leadership learning groups, learning partnerships and school improvement groups.

Micro mobilisation

Although in this chapter we talk about mobilising individuals at a more abstract level, what we are trying to do is mobilise different forms of 'capital' (Hargreaves, 2003) so that they can be used to establish the network. Hargreaves identifies three forms of capital that established networks mobilise: the social, organisational and intellectual. Our view is that during micro mobilisation the network activists need to mobilise those individuals who are the possessors and gatekeepers of these forms of capital:

- *Social (or cultural) capital* – This is the range and quality of a school's connections, both between members of the school, and those beyond it. In establishing a network some schools will have better links with other schools and these might need to be used to help bring these schools on board. Or a school might have an established connection with a local university, or agency, which needs to be drawn into the network.
- *Intellectual capital* – The knowledge within individuals and schools that can be made available to the network. The kind of knowledge required depends upon the foci of the network: it might be of a new initiative the rest of the networks wants to learn about or an established part of one school's practice.
- *Organisational capital* – The knowledge and skill about how to improve schools by making better use of their intellectual and social capital. In our language we would call this leadership capacity and each school will have leaders at different levels who will need to be brought on board to make things happen.

To Hargreaves' list we would want to add a fourth form of capital, 'physical':

- *Physical capital* – These are the material resources, including finance, that are available to schools and that will be made available to others. In the early stages of a network it is surprising the difference that a few hours a week contributed by a good school secretary can make to ensuring that meetings are set up properly and communications run smoothly.

Therefore when thinking of who needs to be 'mobilised' at this stage the activists need to target the key gatekeepers and holders of these various forms of 'capital'. So who needs to be brought on board now to ensure that these various forms of capital will later be shared with the rest of the network?

The recruitment of these key individuals is the aim of micro mobilisation, the first cycle of broadening participation out from the initial group of activists and drawing in the second-wave activists. Micro mobilisation is 'micro' in two senses of the word. First, it is targeted at specific individuals, the key leaders at different levels within schools across the network whose approval or support is needed to release the capital required to allow the network to function. Second, it is 'micro' in the sense that it relies on individual negotiations and is based within the activists' relationships with this key first wave of potential recruits, rather than the 'mass' tactics used later when working across the whole network during macro mobilisation.

In order to help us understand why some networks were more successful than others in mobilising these key leaders, we developed the construct of lateral agency. Lateral agency is the capacity of individuals to work across school boundaries and engage with colleagues in other schools to change their practices. This is a key aspect of the collaborative capacity, the overall ability to work together, we discussed in the previous chapter. Our research into networks, Hadfield *et al.* (2005), showed that lateral agency tends to be easier for individuals to exert on their peers who work in similar positions in other schools. Partially this is a matter of opportunity; groups in the same position within an organisational hierarchy have similar patterns of workload and availability. Peers also tend to share similar responsibilities and problems, so collaboration with them is often intrinsically worthwhile in terms of being able to share concerns and pick up new ideas. There are also cultural issues, in that similar groups share a great deal of common knowledge about the pressures and issues that occupy them.

More successful networks worked strategically so that activists tried to influence others at the same level in school structures, so headteachers set out to influence other headteachers, subject leaders to influence other subject leaders etc. They worked at multiple levels so that not just headteachers were mobilised and they also coordinated working laterally by developing strong vertical structures that supported communication within the activist groups.

But how do these activists exert their lateral agency? In many instances the approaches and techniques were not significantly different to those they used to influence colleagues within their own schools. Working across schools presents additional layers of complexity and challenge. One co-leader neatly summarised the initial leadership challenge faced by those in a new network in working across individual schools, each of which had very different sets of agendas and priorities: 'Seven different schools with seven different sets of priorities, seven different development plans, and what you're trying to do in one network is prioritise one thing that goes across the whole system' (Co-leader, NLC, 2004).

One of the major challenges is that many of the forms of influence available to those working 'vertically' within the hierarchies and structures of their own schools are not available to those working laterally across schools. Lateral agency relies less upon formal power, reward structures and the 'official' status afforded by organisations and much more upon an individual's capacity to directly influence others by developing a relationship with them.

The presence of competing agendas across schools in a network, combined with the need to form a working relationship with other leaders, means that initially activists tend to focus their efforts on consensus building. In these early stages of establishing a network the first area of consensus that needs to be built is about what will be the practical foci and areas of development that will give cohesion to the network. As discussed earlier, a classic mistake by activists is to believe that what motivates them will easily translate across the network as a whole. They fail to recognise that they have to build a focus that is sufficiently motivating to bring on board a critical mass of leaders. The activists' challenge is to gain meaningful rather than just symbolic agreement from key leaders to work collaboratively on an area while ensuring that they do not agree too many or too diverse a set of foci and by so doing undermine the power of working collaboratively.

The process of building consensus is based on constructing a framework within which different groups can work together. As leaders in a variety of contexts face the challenge of building such frameworks it is perhaps unsurprising that some of the most influential research into consensus building took place in studies on 'new' social movements, such as environmental or local campaigns. This is because leaders of such movements have to bring together often fractious smaller organisations into a broader movement to achieve the social changes they seek. Snow *et al.* (1986) in their research within social movements identified a combination of four leadership practices that underpinned consensus building:

- *frame bridging* – providing information to those already disposed to your cause so that they identify with it.
- *frame extension* – where the boundaries of the cause are expanded so that they encompass the agendas of potential recruits.
- *frame amplification* – places emphasis on the compatibility of the values and beliefs of the movement with those of potential members.
- *frame transformation* – involves changing the views of potential recruits so that they align more closely with change agenda being laid out.

Activists in networks may have to engage in all four such practices to develop sufficient consensus across key leaders so that when they mobilise the network it doesn't splinter into several different areas of activity.

The skills and understanding that leaders require to demonstrate this aspect of collaborative capacity can be quite extensive. Frame bridging could be little more than sharing a network plan or it may involve the co-construction of such a plan with several key leaders. Frame extension raises the danger of creating such a broad range of foci that there is insufficient critical mass behind any one initiative within the network. It can be a difficult balancing act deciding on how far the boundaries of a particular focus can be extended while still maintaining cohesion. Frame amplification requires knowledge of other leaders' values and beliefs and it can take considerable time and energy to develop these insights. Frame transformation may also require prolonged engagement with other leaders as activists in the network may have to do more than just a 'selling job', they may have to do an educating one too:

> Well, I've been out to visit some colleagues in their own schools, people who didn't engage . . . So really doing a selling job, explaining how it can enhance the work that's going on in the area. It's a long slow process I think really, I think it's continually re-enforcing the message.
>
> (NLC Annual Inquiry Report, 2004)

Once a degree of consensus has been developed between the initial activists and key leaders, these leaders themselves will have to go through their own cycles of 'micro mobilisation' as they exert their lateral, and vertical, agency to bring yet more people into the network. However many cycles of micro mobilisation are needed once sufficient leadership capacity is in place to access the required levels of capital. Then the 'macro' phase of network building begins, which requires very different strategies and approaches.

Macro mobilisation

If micro mobilisation was marked by the drawing in of key leaders and consensus building, macro mobilisation is based on how to enact the network's initial plans and drawing in larger numbers of practitioners. In our research, Hadfield *et al.* (2005), we make a distinction between the connecting and embedding phases of macro mobilisation. The connecting phase is based on developing structures that draw teachers and other practitioners into working together. A range of structures can be used including:

- joint planning sessions;
- shared professional development activities;
- launch events;
- web sites and forums.

Embedding is marked by the development of the groups that link network and school-based activities. Groups may be brought together because of shared expertise or responsibilities, such as curriculum subject specialists, or school-based professional development coordinators. Such groups are a vital link in engaging those in the classroom with the broader work of the network. These groups and structures need leadership so unsurprisingly one of the most common phenomena during macro mobilisation is the creation of a cohort of middle leaders who are given network-based roles and responsibilities.

Key to a successful macro mobilisation is that those taking on these new leadership roles both establish network processes and create the structures that will sustain them and connect staff across a network. A distinction we make in our research (Hadfield *et al.*, 2004a) is between the leadership 'of' and leadership 'through' network processes. For example, if some form of action enquiry is part of the network then the

> [l]eadership of enquiry will involve setting up and leading research projects or co-ordinating other teachers' work. . . . Leadership through enquiry means developing a process for commissioning enquiry, creating professional development programme for enquiry by external providers, archiving reports, tools and methods, disseminating the findings and making others aware of the network and connecting its work with theirs.
>
> (Hadfield *et al.*, 2004a, p. 5)

In this 'connecting' phase of macro mobilisation it is therefore key that network processes are generative of structures that will support future connections and actions.

These new-wave middle leaders are often given specific titles that indicate their responsibilities within the network so 'lead learners' are common in networks involved in curriculum development, 'school improvement group coordinators' in school improvement networks, as well as more generic terms indicating their overall involvement in leading change, such as 'theme champions'. These roles may grow out of existing school roles that already had a degree of outreach work, as these individuals have often developed the ability to work across school, such as advanced skills teachers, or gifted and talented coordinators.

Vignette: the lead innovator

> We have made a conscious decision to focus early on (in the life of the network) upon adult learning as the route into the other levels of learning. An important part of this has been to adopt an 'invitational' approach to leadership at all levels. The lead innovators were identified as key participants in moving the work of the NLC across schools and in developing 'expertise in their chosen field of school-to-school learning'. By breaking down the 12 schools into smaller groups with focused objectives and specific projects it has been possible to distribute the leadership of network activity through the lead innovators. There has been an element of risk taking for headteachers here, in handing over the project to staff.
>
> The role of the lead innovators has been central in building excitement for the work amongst teachers in the network schools and in moving things forward at the school level . . . the intended role of the lead innovators within the network is to lead development within the school and to coach colleagues in other networked schools. In this way, lead innovators have a role to play in supporting network activity and adult learning across the

network, at the school level, the project group level and at the school-to-school level. In formalising the role of the lead innovators as part of the process of defining roles and responsibilities within the network, it was recognised that they had a key part to play in facilitating progress with the stated outcomes of the NLC.

(Hadfield, 2005, p. 11)

In more mature networks job descriptions were developed for these leadership roles:

Lead Innovators will:
- Develop an action plan for the group (three smaller subsets of schools were formed, each with a different enquiry focus)
- Feed into planning of group/school conferences
- Attend appropriate training
- Inform appropriate Strategic Working Group members responsible for communication, marketing, monitoring and training
- Facilitate appropriate training with schools
- Implement group action plan
- Act as a role model for the initiative
- Share best practice
- Consult children about the success of their learning.

(Hadfield, 2005, p. 12)

This job description reveals another common feature of the work of these middle leaders in this phase of macro mobilisation in that they extended the reach of network activity both vertically and horizontally. Increasing the reach vertically meant not only communicating upwards to the strategic leadership group, but also increasingly drawing in other staff and pupils to participate in the activities of the network. In this instance working horizontally was facilitated by breaking down the network into small sub-networks based on shared developmental foci. Working vertically involved the lead learner in opening up spaces for closer professional dialogues between middle leaders and headteachers:

The network has created an environment in which innovation can take place as a result of the relationships, trust and open dialogue which has been built up. There is a strong focus on professional practice best illustrated in the work of the Lead Innovators. Teachers are now excited and moving things forward in schools and this has presented Headteachers with great opportunities to hear the grass roots perspective on practice. This feels like creating a forum for quality professional dialogue . . . a time to delve into high level professional dialogue.

(Hadfield, 2005, p. 12)

The lead learners had to be supported to cope with the pressure of working across very different contexts; 'training and support for innovative leaders' was provided and groups were supported to develop their 'capacity to generate needs-led INSET' (Hadfield *et al.*, 2004a). They also had to learn how to mediate between the network's focus and the developmental needs of individual schools:

> We recognised that the learning and change that would take place might be different for each school depending on their context and the development of creativity within the curriculum at that time. We believed that it was important that the aims of the project and the nature of change could be facilitated within each of the existing school improvement programmes.
>
> (Hadfield, 2005, p. 12)

In the case of these lead learners, they were able to do this in part because of the emphasis, early on in the network, placed on agreeing common ways of working and developing a shared philosophy about networking:

> Our early meetings were concerned with establishing shared values and principles, we were looking for ways of working so that leadership was distributed in the network and establishing a clear sense of how we would work. The establishment of clear roles and responsibilities here has been key . . . It is a diverse group of schools and because we wanted a shared, non-hierarchical approach there has been lots of talking to come up with a shared philosophy.
>
> (Hadfield, 2005, p. 13)

The embedding part of macro mobilisation comes about through the groups established around key activities developing the reach of the network into the classroom. At this point of establishing the network it is particularly important to have the right people involved in network activities who have sufficient 'clout' – in terms of their status or roles and responsibilities or sufficient 'credibility' – because of their expertise or experience, to convince teachers to change what they do in the classroom. For example, the 'teaching and learning strategy managers' group' established in one network was recognised as requiring the participation of 'the senior person in [each] school, apart from the head, who was leading on teaching and learning' (Hadfield *et al.*, 2004a). This was crucial to the success of the group not only in terms of participants being knowledgeable and able to report on current teaching developments but also having the authority to ensure that network developments impacted on classroom practices in their school.

Just as important as having the right people in these groups is maintaining the correct balance between the number of times these groups meet and what

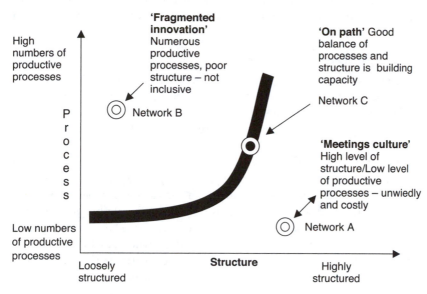

Figure 3.2 The right network flight path

happens when they do. We describe this balance within the network as 'the flight path' (see Figure 3.2). This is because if you get the balance right the network will take off, get it wrong and it will never leave the ground. The correct network flight path is when the balance between structures, in this phase the frequency of meetings and events, and processes, the quality and effectiveness of what people do when they come together, interact to generate further connections while maintaining cohesion amongst those involved. If at the beginning the network becomes too highly structured and insufficiently productive, whether in terms of new learning or connections, then the network devolves into a meetings culture where no one can really see what they are getting out of it. If though there is insufficient structure but it is marked out by highly productive processes then this may lead to fragmented developments in which a great deal of energy is dissipated for no sustained impact.

In Figure 3.2 Network A has fallen into the trap of over-emphasising structures rather than developing productive processes. This means that network members meet frequently but insufficient thought has been given to what they are getting from the network, whether in terms of professional development or contacts. Groups quickly descend into administration and 'business' meetings with little personal learning. The meetings lack a variety of approaches and staff attendance falls off. This is because this network has developed a 'meetings' rather than a 'learning' culture. In contrast, Network B has multiple learning processes going on which are highly engaging for a small number of enthusiastic staff. Unfortunately, there is insufficient co-ordination to allow learning to be shared between the different groups or in a concerted manner back in school:

> There are little bombs going off every day. The task in the next 18 months is to embed it and widen it, and it's got to be co-ordinated. It's made a difference to us and it's made a difference to our children but it's got to make a difference everywhere.
>
> (Lead learner, quoted in Hadfield and Jopling, 2007)

In contrast, Network C has got the balance right between the degree of structure and the number of these processes. They have managed to get the dynamic right so that they can coordinate an increasing number of learning and coordinating processes without increasing greatly the number of structures. If this point is achieved the network will start to generate additional capacity which is not being absorbed into maintaining structures but instead is developing new processes which will sustain its work in the future. For example, teachers involved in action enquiry in each school are now able to teach and mentor new staff about enquiry without having to use external expertise or create a whole new structure. Middle leaders who initially supported the enquiry groups in their schools will pass on this expertise to other middle leaders who are leading different processes. In addition network and school structures are starting to become integrated and there is far less duplication of meetings.

Keeping on the correct 'path' and getting the balance right is particularly important while establishing a school network. Schools cannot afford the luxury of too much individual or collaborative learning that doesn't make an impact back in the classroom, nor can they waste time and energy in too many meetings. The external accountability systems that surround schools will often need to be convinced of the worth of any collaborative activity and this, and other pressures, leaves them with little room for error in how they engage in networking. Networks are always open to criticisms of being 'the mediocre teaching the mediocre', lacking in powerful learning processes, or only being for the committed few. There is probably no ideal mix, but activists and leaders have to be careful about creating too restrictive or expansive a structure while avoiding the situation where a great deal of unconnected activity is taking place.

Being on the right flight path is not only a matter of the number of structures that are developing but also whether they are the right ones. Structures need to develop that can support the range of processes needed to ensure that collaborative learning and collective action results in changes in classrooms. There are three broad types of processes that need to be under-pinned by effective structures:

- *Joint learning* – These events are opportunities for learning from each other or from external experts and can range from shared CPD activities to cross-school action research groups.
- *Joint planning* – The planning here may be for further network activity or joint work in schools. It is important that joint planning does eventually focus in on school- and classroom-based changes.
- *Joint working* – Just as with joint planning, working together needs eventually to focus in on the classroom otherwise the network simply becomes a 'talking shop' in which nothing has an impact on pupils.

To be generative at the level of the network these processes need to work across schools and this may require a range of structures. These structures can vary from a programme of inter-visitations, a network-wide conference to a formal coaching and mentoring scheme. Some of the most common types of structures used in networks are presented in Table 3.2 on the following page.

No one process or structure is more likely to lead to a network 'taking off' than any other, more importantly it is how these productive structures and processes are combined that is the key. Leaders of networks need to use various combinations of these different structures, and monitor the flow of activity they generate, in order to facilitate learning between schools that moves staff into joint planning and work that impacts in classroom. In our research (Hadfield *et al.*, 2004b), networks that reported using only one structure had far lower levels of impact than those that had been engaged in a number of school-to-school processes at different levels.

In the following vignette a network in the embedding stage developed its own strategic approach to professional development that eventually impacted within classrooms.

Vignette: using a range of CPD processes to establish a network

This network of 12 primary schools was grouped into four triads to create planned opportunities for shared inter-dependent professional development. Each triad focused on a different issue:

- time to talk;
- problem solving skills in maths;
- enhancing children's talk;
- developing independent learning.

Lead teachers in each school were provided with a short training programme, and on-going support, by an experienced action researcher from a local university. They undertook individual action research projects and then they and their colleagues held twilight meetings with staff from other schools in their triad to share their experiences, the outcomes of the research and to plan

Table 3.2 Generative structures that support collaboration between schools

Direction and flow of structure	Range of structures	Example of how one of these structures underpins key learning processes	Its impact on individuals, schools and networks
One school to one school	Mentoring and coaching schemes, research lessons study programmes, peer observation schemes.	Having a network mentor/coach – The mentor can provide new ideas and practice from elsewhere. They can motivate practitioners to seek new knowledge and become involved in further learning.	'Because I was one of the teacher practitioners seconded last year it gave me instant access to other networks which was enormously helpful and because [X] mentored and coached me that was enormously helpful as well ... It made me very curious. I wanted to find out more' (Teacher).
One school to many schools	Programmes of inter-visitations, critical friendships, school-based consultants.	Undertaking inter-visitations – A programme of visits to a school that has developed an area of expertise can inspire a groups of staff from other schools to establish their own innovations.	'[T]his trip to was offered to the link teachers ... it was just an inspiration ... we all came back on the train and we were saying "what are we going to do next", so we set up our own thinking skills group within the network' (Deputy headteacher).
Many schools to one school	Sustained programmes of professional development or enquiry support delivered by school teams.	Regular teacher researcher meetings – These provided a mixture of support and pressure for novice researchers from some schools by creating peer pressure to complete individual enquiry activity and help in feeding back into schools.	'The very fact that you're involved with other people in the network means that there's a good reason to keep the momentum going. In terms of research, you can't allow the inertia to build up because you've made a commitment to it' (Assistant principal).
Many schools to many schools	Network-wide conferences (including pupil voice). Cross-phase and theme groups, enquiry groups, subject specialist groups. Network-based enquiry and action research groups	Network 'pupil voice' conference – Enthusiasm and positive feedback from pupils involved can in turn inspire teachers in other schools to become more actively involved in the network.	'[T]he children [in the network] have met regularly and the staff who have worked with the children have been fired up and motivated by the children's enthusiasm' (Network leader).

follow-up work. The teacher-researchers shared their work with each other and all the heads from the network in a joint seminar, which was a 'key moment' – 'the network became united, excited by the quality and findings of the research'.

Findings were disseminated through staff meetings and a variety of other events, such as a parents' maths evening and a learning support assistant training programme. Joint working also took the form of a story-telling day, where approximately 1,000 children and 60 staff worked together, and a pupil voice conference.

By structuring itself into smaller sub-networks, based on shared themes, this network was able to cut down on the complexity of meetings but still provide opportunities for staff to learn and plan together. They also created a range of opportunities for staff not directly involved, and parents and other pupils, to become aware of the work and to take it further, thus giving the network a pretty good 'flight plan'.

Summary

Establishing a network involves cycles of mobilisation moving out from the 'seed' of initial activist. In its initial stages this is about bringing on board those who can help mobilise the various types of capital the network will need. Once sufficient leadership capacity has been brought into the network then the macro mobilisation, in which the basic processes and structures are established, can begin. The groups of new middle leaders who take on network leadership roles are the link between these two stages. Having being recruited during the previous stage it is these leaders who ensure that the network stays on the right flight path.

The development of leadership capacity needs to be planned for strategically as the network moves out from the initial set of activities to key leaders and beyond. It involves the development and utilisation of different forms of agency, structures and processes all of which need to be aligned and coordinated if the network is to 'take-off'. The network becomes established at this point when it is no longer the property of the activists who started it and starts to influence a critical mass of practitioners.

Tool 3.1: agreeing foci

A crucial first stage in the micro mobilisation process is developing consensus amongst key leaders as to the foci of collaborative activity. Developing such a consensus is an on-going process and has to move through the various layers of a network, from activists and key leaders through to middle leaders. The following tool will help leaders and activists at all levels consider their network foci and question why it has come about.

The tool represents the process of developing a focus as akin to moving through a series of funnels that gradually narrow down the selection, but at

Guidance on key issues involved in building a network

Micro mobilisation	Courting	The motivations and purposes that draw activists into a network are likely to be very different than those that will engage other key leaders. The activists' challenge is to gain meaningful rather than just symbolic agreement from other leaders. Consensus building can be achieved by frame bridging, extension, amplification, and transformation.
	Aligning	Lateral agency is the capacity of individuals to work across school boundaries and engage with colleagues in other schools and change their practices. It is easier to exert pressure on peers who work in similar positions in other schools. Effective networks ensure that leaders at a range of levels within schools connect across to other schools so that mobilisation is not restricted to certain tiers. Lateral agency is important for influencing peers in other schools, but vertical coordination of the network is also key.
Macro mobilisation	Connecting	The middle leaders who take responsibility for developing the earliest network processes need to use these to build the key network structures. In this phase it is important that network activity is generative of structures that will support future connections and actions. The key generative processes are joint learning, joint planning and joint work.
	Embedding	The correct network flight path is when there is a balance between structures, the frequency of meetings and events, and processes, the quality and effectiveness of what people do when they come together. No one process or structure is more likely to lead to a network 'taking off' than any other. More importantly it is how these productive structures and processes are combined that is the key. Joint planning and working together needs eventually to focus in on the classroom otherwise the network simply becomes a 'talking shop' in which nothing has an impact on pupils.

the end of each funnel the options widen again before again being narrowed down. This is a visual way of representing how at certain points options expand and then later become more focused. These expansions and contractions occur because of the movement brought about by a fundamental tension in selecting a focus (Figure 3.3).

This tension encapsulates the shifts that individuals in the network will go through as they move between moments of consensus building when they

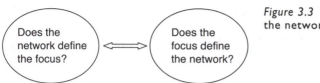

Figure 3.3 What came first, the network or the focus?

define the foci and then moments of buy-in as they opt to work on a certain foci rather than another.

Moving down through these funnels is based on the idea that in developing foci across different groups it is important to recognise that they will go through a number of stages and understand where each of them are at anyone time. These stages can be represented by a series of questions:

1   What do we want to do as a network?
2   What do we need to do as a network?
3   How can we respond as a network?
4   How should we respond as a network?

These stages represent a movement from wants to needs and a shift in thinking about how to respond from ideas based on what the network can currently do to a more considered response based on the existing knowledge base around an area.

Tool 3.2: mapping mobilisation

This tool is based on creating a form of organ-o-gram of the network being built. This is a diagrammatic representation of the key processes and structures within it. When done in sufficient detail it should provide the leaders of the network with a skeleton overview of what they are building, and are intending to build.

The best way of using this tool is as a way of creating a shared understanding of the network with others and as a means of monitoring its development over time. Therefore this task is most productive when it is done as a group activity and when it is repeated at regular intervals and comparisons made with the previous versions.

A key point at which to create the first organ-o-gram is when the network is moving from micro to macro mobilisation. At this point certain structures and processes are in place and more are about to be created. Developing this kind of strategic overview with the key leaders who have been recruited during the first stages of micro mobilisation gives them the opportunity to understand the network more holistically and their role and position within it, as well as that of their staff and school. As important as the process of developing the diagrammatic overview is the discussion of it that follows.

Moving from wants to needs

Collecting wants and wishes – The first stage is to collect together those areas people would like to work on. In the first instance these are likely to be established ideas, drawn from individual organisational plans, or forthcoming issues that could be the result of new external policies.

How you draw together these wants and wishes depends on the degree of trust and common knowledge that exists in the network. Where high levels exist it may be a case of simply discussing school plans in a meeting. Where low levels are present it may require an external facilitator to collect issues from headteachers and process them into possible areas of collaboration.

Theme into issues – The next stage is to group potential foci together. This can require some work as; 'solution' based foci may appear without the actual 'problem' being clearly articulated, different terms being used for the same issues, and some foci being more specific versions of other broader ones. A good starting point is to circulate the emerging themes and issues around the network and ask head-teachers and senior leaders to look for possible connec-tions.

What do we need to collaborate on? – At this point certain themes may appear around which people will want to collaborate. The next big question is 'What issues are best dealt with collaboratively? What are best dealt with individually?' This forces a consideration of what the potential benefits are of working together. Those foci that *need* people to collaborate on will be the most powerful organisers. Those where people are likely to see immediate benefits will make it easier to keep some leaders involved.

What could we do? – By now the network should have decided upon a single focus, or a small number, which have relevance to all the schools and around which they can work. But how to work collaboratively around the foci? Again it is important in the consensus building process to generate options about how to pro-ceed. At this point key leaders are going to be developing a long list of potential processes and interventions they would like to make. This will reveal differences in preferred ways of working and levels of prior experiences with certain approaches.

Defining your focus

Figure 3.4 Defining a focus for your network

Moving from 'coulds' to 'shoulds'

Additional possibilities – It may be the case that alternative responses will need to be generated by connecting with the existing knowledge base around an issue. This may involve using existing professional networks to look at how other schools and networks have approached similar developments. It may though require a more comprehensive search by contacting national agencies, consultants, active researchers and local universities.

The list of possible 'coulds' should now be a relatively rich mixture of possible approaches, processes, materials, projects and interventions. Not all of these possibilities will be worth further development and at this point some will be disregarded. For those worth further consideration additional information needs to be collected concerning their effectiveness and costs. This might involve site visits to schools, consultations with academics and researchers and reviews of the existing literature.

The movement of possible 'coulds' to becoming 'shoulds' starts with them being assessed against a series of criteria concerned with their effectiveness, applicability to your particular network, and cost of implementation. The specifics of these criteria will depend upon the processes and the nature of the network, and also its stage of development. A new network may wish to select interventions and processes that generate relatively quick impacts and so help convince others of the value of collaboration. In practice it is not just a question of selecting a single process or intervention but also considering how they might combine. Some may be in-depth innovations that will take time to mature but potentially could have a profound impact, while others will be more widespread and immediate but will have more superficial impacts on practitioners and learners.

The foci will need to be renegotiated at several levels and points across the network. It therefore needs to be in a form which is transferable. One successful approach has been to develop the foci in a form somewhere between enquiry questions and learning objectives.

We know 'W' so how can we use 'X' to do 'Y' to create 'Z'? – We know that peer assessment and questioning can improve learning (W), so how can we use our coaching expertise (X) to enable pupils to assess their learning (Y) as to create a better understanding and articulation of their own learning (Z)?

We know that schools in our network are experiencing increasing levels of within-year pupil mobility and that this is affecting the learning capacity and energy of schools, teachers and pupils in the network (W). So how can we use the research evidence on mobility and transition (X) to improve systems and skills across the network for assessing and achievement tracking individual pupils (Y) in order to minimise learning loss (Z)?

The task

There are three parts to the task:

1   Completing a network grid.
2   Drawing the organ-o-gram.
3   Discussion and review.

Completing a network grid

Before drawing the overview of the network it is important to consider the key processes and structures within it that need to be represented in the diagram. The grid helps you collect this information systematically and to pool it before you actually start to draw the network. You can then check at the end of the process that everything that should be included is represented. Filling in the grid is also a useful way of reviewing who is involved in what activity and will help you start to answer the first major question. An example of a network grid is provided at the end of this tool (Table 3.3).

HAVE WE GOT THE RIGHT PEOPLE INVOLVED SO FAR?

Table 3.3 gives you an outline of the information that you need to collect and represent in the diagram. You might want to circulate this grid partially completed, or at least with the first column filled in, prior to bringing the key leaders together so they can add the detail from their perspective. The information they provide can then be collated before you try and represent the network visually.

Drawing the organ-o-gram

There are various ways of visualising a network that range across a dimension, at one end of which are more metaphorical images, a tree with roots and spreading branches, to the other end which is more diagrammatic, for example a flow chart. In creating an organ-o-gram you can choose at which end of this dimension you want to be but being too extreme at either end will create problems. You may well feel the network is akin to a polar bear afloat on an iceberg but this image is probably not going to help others understand its format and structure. On the other hand trying to represent the network as an elaborate wiring diagram or your own version of the London tube system is also unlikely to be helpful. At the end of this task we have provided a gallery of network structures that might be helpful (Figure 3.5).

A common starting point to developing an organ-o-gram is to draw in the strategic leadership groups and then work outwards from there. Some people prefer to put these key groups on small cards so they can be moved around on a larger sheet before deciding on their relationship with each other. The relationship between groups can be expressed by their physical position to each other and by how they are linked, which can be represented by using various types of lines and words.

If you have a large group of people working you can split them into smaller teams and each can try and develop their own representation. At the end of which you create a 'gallery' and vote on which seems to be the best representation of the network.

Discussion and review

Once the organ-o-gram is complete it is important to discuss it and use it to review how the network has developed to date. The review should move through a series of stages from specific to increasingly holistic issues and questions.

1   Appropriateness of individual processes and structures:
    • Are the key processes likely to deliver the aims we have for them?
    • Are they structured appropriately – in terms of make up of the groups and the frequency with which they meet?
    • Have we got good connection between the network structures and in-school structures?

2   Linkages between various processes and structures:
    • Could we simplify the number of groups by getting them involved in different processes?
    • Have we linked up the right groups and processes?
    • Do we have enough vertical coordination as well as lateral?

3   Overview of the whole network:
    • Have we got the overall balance right between processes and structures?
    • Are any schools or key groups not connected properly?
    • Are the processes and groups going to build on each other's work or conflict?
    • What do we see as the weakest links?

GALLERY

If you only have one group creating a organ-o-gram then the final part of the discussion task, when you are reviewing the network, can be developed by using this Gallery activity. It can also be used when you have more than one group once they have selected their preferred representation of their network. The aim of this task is to present network leaders with a range of different network models, get them to consider the pros and cons of each, and then to critically consider the strengths and weaknesses of their own network.

All you need to do is photocopy or project onto an interactive whiteboard the following examples, and see which example people think most closely resembles their network and if they feel it shares similar advantages and disadvantages.

Table 3.3 A network grid

Key aims and major processes that underpin them Identify under each major aim the main generative processes that will achieve them.	Structures within each process Identify the key groups, individuals and institutions that are involved within each of the major processes. Some groups may appear more than once.	Core purposes of groups and individuals • Developing enquiry and transfer of practice • Coordination and planning (e.g. developing strategy, reviewing) • Developing people and process (e.g. training, mentoring)	Flow, scope and membership Do they work one to one, one to many etc.? Are they attempting to work across the network or in just a few schools? Who is in the group?	Connects to . . . e.g. how and to whom does this group connect?	Frequency Number of meetings per term
Already in existence					
Planned but not initiated					

Figure 3.5 Gallery of network structures

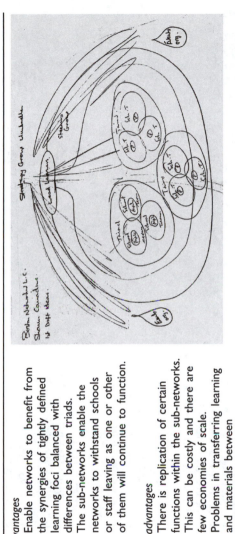

Sub-network structure
On a day-to-day basis the network effectively operates as a series of sub-networks. The sub-networks only meet periodically as a whole group.

Advantages
• Enable networks to benefit from the synergies of tightly defined learning foci balanced with differences between triads.
• The sub-networks enable the networks to withstand schools or staff leaving as one or other of them will continue to function.

Disadvantages
• There is replication of certain functions within the sub-networks. This can be costly and there are few economies of scale.
• Problems in transferring learning and materials between sub-networks.

Figure 3.5 Continued

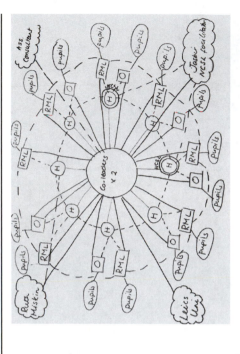

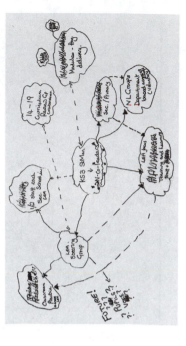

Wheel and spoke
Leadership sits at the
centre of a web of activists.
Groups of school-based
teachers focus on their
individual schools, but also
meet as a network-wide
group. Their work is
disseminated at network
conferences.

Advantages
• Work is likely to have high
  degree of personal meaning for
  individual teachers.
• A critical mass of teachers can be
  involved and this gives economies
  of scale and may mean it is
  possible to secure external
  support, i.e. from local university
  or local authority.

Disadvantages
• Unless the work of individuals is
  connected to an interested
  steering group or a within school
  structure it may not be taken up
  by others and so fail to impact
  outside of their classroom or school.

Externally facilitated networks
Network is facilitated by an
external group such as a
university or the local
education authority.
The external group provide
the majority of the
day-to-day leadership and
the network operates largely
detached from headteachers.

Advantages
• The leadership has dedicated
  time to facilitate the network
  giving it considerable additional
  capacity.

Disadvantages
• Without headteacher engagement,
  long-term sustainability may be
  limited.
• The network itself may become
  detached from the school
  development plans.

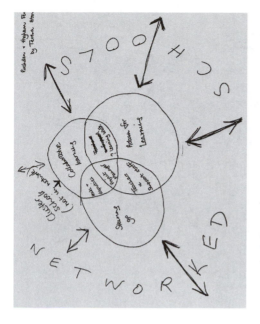

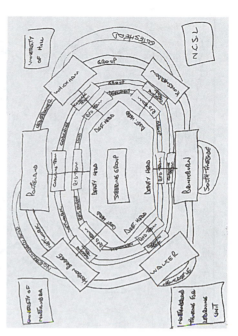

Integrated networks

Limited number of network groups but with a high degree of overlapping membership.

For example, steering group is comprised of enquiry group leaders.

Advantages

- Tight linkage between the network's strategic and operational functions.
- Can make the best use of limited leadership capacity.

Disadvantages

- The highly overlapping network groups may limit reach.
- The existing leadership capacity may quickly become burnt out.

Concentric networks

With a steering group that reports to a strategy group at the centre, the network of schools is intercrossed with a range of different role-based or theme groups – a headteachers' group, research groups, learning support assistants' groups, for example.

Advantages

- Network groups have well-defined roles which provide focus and direction that prevents them becoming distracted. For example, headteacher learning groups ensures they do not become consumed with administrative work.
- The range of different groups criss-crossing schools gives the network a high profile.

Disadvantages

- These resource-hungry networks may drain leadership capacity from the schools.

Figure 3.5 Continued

Thematic or role-based networks

Network configures around practitioners with similar roles, such as newly qualified teachers, or project groups are convened to address particular cross-curricular issues – for example, thinking skills, assessment for learning, or pupil voice. The theme groups may organise workshops or conferences. In larger networks, particular themes may have their own steering groups.

Advantages

- Strong synergies can be built from a tight learning focus.
- Can draw in highly subject-specific expertise.
- May provide room for specialised areas of personally appealing and professionally relevant work that would be unavailable within another school.
- A shared foci with a critical mass of experienced people can create strong communities of practice.

Disadvantages

- Where the network is based on particular roles, it may seem somewhat exclusive.
- Schools can be overloaded by too many initiatives.

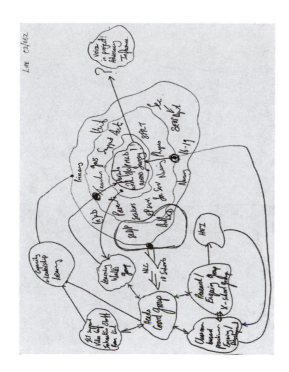

Process-based networks

These networks adopt one or a very limited number of processes which domiate their strcture. They tend to focus on activities that can be used across the network for a range of ends. This would include activities such as a network enquiry based on a programme of inter-visitations or a group of subject specialists from across the network using research lessons.

Advantages

- By establishing good processes the network facilitates effective outcomes.

Disadvantages

- Processes that are cascaded down may become diluted.

Figure 3.5 Continued

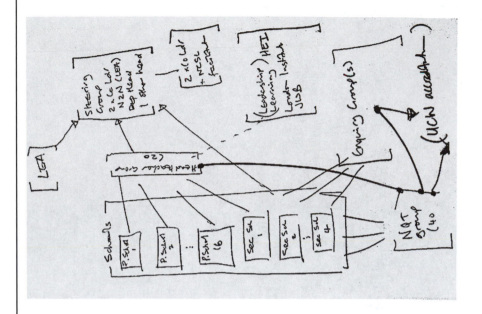

Cross-phase networks
Networks involving both primary and secondary school networks. Varying in level of collaboration depending on learning focus. Collaboration emerges from broadly defined foci of general relevance (e.g. thinking skills, enquiry methods) or areas of interdependence such as transition.

Advantages
• Increased cross-phase understanding may have huge benefits for pupils in transition.

Disadvantages
• Secondary schools may dominate primary schools.
• Network may be characterised by disjunction and exist as mechanism to access networked funding.

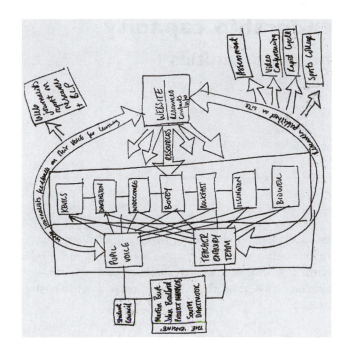

Virtual or 'light-touch' networks
Network has few persistent groups. Instead, a central coordinating group brings together short-lived project groups. A great deal of network members communicate through, or draw resources and reports down from, a website or bulletin board.

Advantages
- Has the opportunity to allow teachers at the periphery of the network to become involved and access materials.
- Allows a dynamic and resource-light approach to networking

Disadvantages
- Can lack opportunities to develop relationships; practitioners may have no sense of ownership over the network.
- Without a history of relationships and trust between schools.
- Infrastructure costs may not warrant levels of participation.

Chapter 4

Building leadership capacity
Challenges and opportunities

Introduction

In the previous chapter we explored a number of issues and challenges associated with getting a network started. In this chapter we move on to consider issues of leadership and management, and in particular how leadership capacity can be developed within and across networks. This chapter sets out to answer the following questions:

- Why do we need 'network leaders' and what are their qualities?
- What do successful network leaders do?
- How do network leaders build leadership capacity within and across networks?
- What are the key challenges network leaders face?

We answer these questions by drawing on insights from existing network leaders, by sharing with you some of the tools we have developed during our work, and by again providing you with short accounts of networks we have come across in our own research.

Why do we need 'network leaders' and what are their qualities?

First, let's turn our attention to the notion of what we mean by network leadership. To understand this term and to get a grasp what kind of leadership it encompasses we need to remind ourselves of the context from which it has emerged. During recent years school leaders have faced unparalleled challenges; they have been expected to develop organisations with the flexibility to cope with increasingly wide-ranging demands (Hargreaves, 2003). Demands in the UK, and in many other contexts, have ranged from traditional within-school activities, including focusing on maximising the quality of teaching and learning, providing guidance for staff development and ensuring clear policies and structures are in place to support a healthy learning environment, to those which move school leaders outside of their traditional educational concerns to engage with broader social and cultural issues. In the UK recent policy developments, such as the Every Child Matters and Extended Schools agendas, have led to the development of a 'well-being' agenda that takes a holistic view of children's development in which education plays its part alongside issues of physical safety and emotional and social development. This more integrated view of children's needs has been responded to by a rise of multi-agency approaches in which schools have shifted, and been shifted, to the centre of the provision of children's services within local communities. Similar demands and shifts can be found in other countries where the rise of full-service schools and community schooling have been just some of the responses.

As challenges develop and complex agendas emerge schools are changing with many recognising their limitations for themselves and proactively setting out to develop and renegotiate relationships with a broad range of partners, viewing themselves as part of an interconnected mini-system rather than a stand-alone organisation. Others have needed to be pushed in this direction.

Just as schools and local education systems are having to respond to these challenges so is our understanding of what we mean by leadership. We are working towards a situation where networking and collaboration across traditional boundaries have rapidly become the orthodoxy for generating change to deliver excellent and equitable outcomes within our system. This is particularly evident in terms of challenging underachievement and persistent school failure. Clearly, this has significant implications for school leaders and those involved in schools and education more widely (Chapman and Fullan, 2007). In the UK this has given rise to the discussion of 'system leaders' or 'system leadership' (PWC, 2007). Put simply, this refers to leaders who have the ability to operate beyond their own organisations and have the ability to influence the leadership of others. It is our view that network leadership is distinct from system leadership because system leadership remains premised on the notion of systems based on traditional organisations and leadership that operates primarily within their hierarchical structures.

In contrast we believe that network leadership is not based within the structures of traditional organisations, rather it lies within the networks of relationships and collaborative practices that mark out the new emergent system. It is a form of leadership that moves easily between the individualism of system leadership to the more social forms of distributed leadership. This is because network leadership resides within individuals and groups and is expressed in both individual and collective agency. Its primary purpose is to lead development and coordinate activity laterally or horizontally across the network rather than vertically to influence the system. Herein lies the key challenge of network leadership. Leaders are expected to lead without formal power or authority over their colleagues; a situation quite different from traditional forms of school leadership. Therefore, the skills and relationships necessary to implement change are quite different from and arguably more sophisticated than those associated with traditional school settings where, for example, if and when necessary, a line manager can mandate change. In most network settings, even those that are formalised to a degree, leaders are still highly dependent upon certain aspects of voluntarism, for example with regard to macro mobilisation of those who are not directly connected with the network. For example, a trust school has sought to develop a network including a university and further education college. The principal and other senior leaders have negotiated the university and trust's involvement to support the vision of establishing lifelong learning in an area of severe socio-economic deprivation. Mobilising these institutions and those within the community connected with it will require individual brokerage and mass mobilisation, a complex mixture of individual and collective agency. Network leaders will on an individual basis find themselves using skills of negotiation, brokerage, facilitation and disturbance-handling, often within highly politi-cised environments where agendas and the balance of power and influence are unclear. They will also be operating collectively with others where issues of framing, mobilising participation and coordination of collective actions will be key.

One way of considering this complex mix of individual leadership skills and aptitudes, collective actions and group processes that define network leadership is to consider them as a series of different intelligences. In previous research we identified in successful school-to-school partnership and collaboration that individual leaders and groups had strengths in particular areas (Chapman *et al.*, 2006). These strengths or *intelligences* spanned a range of technical and social capacities. They included:

- *Contextual intelligence* – A detailed understanding of the environment, the key factors that constitute the environment and the interplay between them. Put simply, what is it that makes the network community unique?
- *Social intelligence* – The ability to relate to people and generate social capital. Put simply, an understanding of the people involved in the network and their values, needs and motivations.
- *Pragmatic intelligence* – An optimistic but realistic perspective on people and events. Put simply, an understanding of what the network can achieve.
- *Leadership intelligence* – The ability to shape and mould organisational ethos. Put simply, an understanding of how to hold the network together and to move it forward.
- *Management intelligence* – An appreciation of the importance of effective structure and coordination. Put simply, an understanding of what network routines need to be in place to facilitate action.

This framework is a powerful one for considering the leadership capacity of any network because an assessment of these intelligences can be either individual or collective.

It is not only important that network leaders have these intelligences but that they know when and how to draw on them as a resource to influence change. Second, they should understand the inter-relationship between the different intelligences. It is not simply a case of knowing when and how to draw on them; network leadership requires them to be combined and the interplay between them is vital. Combining them may require a rapid movement from more individualistic to distributed notions of leadership, from an individual to a group, and back again. Finally, effective network leadership will also set out to develop such intelligences within both individuals and groups.

It is difficult to unpack each of these intelligences in one chapter but let's take a look at a key one, contextual intelligence, and take a fundamental aspect of that, an understanding of the motivations behind why people might work together in a network. In our research we have looked at how leaders in networks read those they are working with and the motivations, or drivers, that push people towards collaborating, and we have analysed these using a framework adapted from Sullivan and Skelcher (2003). There are basically three broad categories: pessimists, optimists and realists.

Pessimists engage in collaboration through selfishness or motives related to empire building. Here leaders refuse to engage in networks unless engagement preserves or enhances their power. This perspective is based on the transaction of resources, fulfilling programme requirements and maintenance of power, position and generally preserving the status quo. In contrast optimists engage in collaboration because they believe it will result in gains for the system as a whole, and that the altruism of stakeholders will override the desire for individual organisational gains. Realists adopt a position where altruism and individual gain can co-exist. Here leaders view the wider environment, specifically the changing context, as the driver for collaboration. For Sullivan and Skelcher (2003, p. 41) the focus is on 'how either or both can be achieved through collaborative activity in the changing context' rather than what or when.

Our work has taken us to many networks and collaborations where leaders have held largely pessimistic perspectives. These networks may have a leader(s) who enthuses about their collaborative work and the additional benefits belonging to the network brings to their school. These network leaders often have good plans on paper but when you scratch below the surface there is nothing there, these are empty networks. Importantly, ownership and involvement tend to be limited, these network leaders neglect to build leadership capacity. Leaders tend to prefer to invest their time and energy into securing and maximising (what they perceive as) their share of resources and demonstrate they have done what has been required of them by an external agency. Alternatively, some leaders choose to become silent partners, drawing down their allocation of resource and using it for their own purposes without engaging the network at all. These networks tend to be dependent on funding streams and often dissolve when additional resources dry up. They also tend to unravel when an enthusiast or key individual moves on. In short, network leaders who subscribe to the pessimistic perspective are destined to fail before they start; these networks usually wither and die with little or no impact beyond the acquisition of a few laptops or other capital investment.

We have also spent much time in networks where leaders held optimistic perspectives. These networks tend to be very different. Leaders in these networks often have a strong commitment to the other members of the network and the network as a whole. Unlike network leaders holding pessimistic perspectives these network leaders tend to have plans in place but are always trying to move beyond them and expand network activity. For these network leaders there is no sense of going through the actions to get the resource. Rather, those involved have a strong sense of self-efficacy and are exposed to a new range of skills and experiences that help to build leadership capacity within individuals across the network, but it tends to be limited to a group of enthusiasts who are committed to networking as a process. Network leaders can tend to the evangelical and may be tinged with a sense of self-gratification – *they are part of the network because it is the right thing to do*. Despite the fact these leaders are often excellent at using school-based and other data to generate evidence-informed practice, for some, networking is a blind spot where the desire to collaborate seems to cloud their judgement. This can lead to complacency and a lack of criticality where the network becomes the focus for all activity and is seen as a panacea. Ultimately, these networks are also destined to failure, although they may wither and die at a slower rate or be temporarily revived by an influx of new blood who share the optimistic perspective or implementation of a new initiative. These networks can bounce from one initiative to another irrespective of whether the initiative is attached to resources.

The most successful networks are those in which a majority of leaders adopt a realist perspective. They tend to be driven by a strong sense of moral purpose and wanting to do the best for the communities they serve. They resist the temptation to view the network as a panacea but they believe the network is a worthwhile entity and use data to evaluate impact and guide development. As individuals, successful network leaders show and demand professional generosity. This often forms the basis of trusting relationships. By this we mean they are prepared to share their staff for the benefit of other schools even at a difficult time for their own school, or when it may lead to losing the individual through promotion or another professional opportunity elsewhere. The attitude of these leaders is that there will be another individual with equal talent to replace them and if not they will develop one. This selflessness promotes the building of social capital across the network that further reinforces linkages between those directly involved and creates opportunities for drawing others in to create clusters of new relationships. As this evolves, individuals and groups inhabit new spaces, facing new challenges and taking on new roles and responsibilities. As spaces are inhabited, spaces are also vacated. These spaces also provide opportunities for individuals and groups to take on new roles and responsibilities within and across the network. For example, as a pastoral specialist in one school may take on a new role across the network, some of their pastoral role within the school can be used to induct another member of staff in leading a strand of pastoral activity to gain leadership experience of pastoral issues. This is *real* distributed leadership, where leadership opportunities emerge organically, both formally and informally, within member organisations and across the network. Such opportunities, underpinned by formation of new relationships and individuals moving around the network, are integral to building leadership capacity.

Being able to take a critical view of the motivations of those you are collaborating with is an important aspect of contextual intelligence and it needs to be utilised when assessing not only the leadership culture within the strategic leadership but also at all levels within a network. Individuals will find similar differences in motivation within their own schools and dealing with these is key to managing staff buy-in and mobilising them to engage with the network.

What do successful network leaders do?

The following vignettes, describing a soft federation and extended school-based network, illustrate the application of a number of these intelligences by effective network leaders.

Vignette: management and contextual intelligences

The soft federation is composed of one secondary and two primary schools and the extended network involves 11 feeder primary schools across an area of 300 square miles. In terms of leadership and management structures within the federation each school retains its own governance and leadership but has streamlined its governing bodies and dissolved all committees. Three representatives from each school sit on the federation's strategic committee. The relationships between the federation schools and wider network are underpinned and guided by a jointly developed mission statement based on the eight conditions for raising student aspirations as defined by the Global Institute for Student Aspirations (GISA).

In an attempt to enhance the operational and strategic running within the secondary school and to better coordinate network activity the head decided to reduce the weekly senior management team meetings to a membership of five to tackle routines and 'to ensure basic things are operational'. However, overall the senior management team has been widened, with each member having their own dedicated areas of focus; working in a series of small sub-groups on specific particular issues. This allows leadership to be spread across more staff with most involved in whole-school and federation/network issues. The network itself has also been a driver for expanding the leadership team, 'as more initiatives have been taken on, there has been the invitation to more staff to become leadership people'. This is viewed as a flexible system, which can easily be modified when more schools decide to join in with the networking opportunities provided by the federation. As the federation develops it may be that arrangements become more formalised. Should the move to a 'hard' federation take place, the head (and other colleagues) expect the leadership structure to operate with an executive head located in one school and with the deputy overseeing the two primary partner schools. It may be that primary headteachers may also lead small groups of three or four schools. Then each primary school would have a curriculum leader. A senior manager reflected:

> It would be fantastic if we could have an executive head and a management structure that worked seamlessly across the schools . . . to have assistant heads, deputy heads who are literally working in both schools, managing aspects in both schools.

In this network all levels of staff are involved, from senior leaders who tend to provide strategic leadership and act as advocates for the federation and extended network to teachers, support staff and administrators. Networking activity includes collaborative work relating to subject continuity and transition: 'we do a lot of joint planning work'. The head and chair of governors were felt to be the combined driving force for the network and the move towards federation. They are credited with responsibility for the vision and enthusiasm to drive the developments. The chair of governors 'has been instrumental in making this very straight forward'. 'Without the leadership from the top it couldn't happen.'

Some may view school-based networks and particularly soft federations as the first of a series of incremental steps towards becoming fully integrated or a merger. Therefore, such collaborations may be considered suspicious or even threatening. In this case the main barrier to collaborating was the feeder primary schools fearing a loss of identity or autonomy. The secondary headteacher acknowledged this and spent much time and energy managing the expectations and clearly defining boundaries with the partner primary schools. The headteacher reflected: 'they were keen to keep their personal identity and I completely support that . . . individual identity will be protected and indeed cherished'. Another barrier was identified as being the fear of change:

> it's either the head is very close to retirement and doesn't want to rock the boat or it's people who want to move forward in the county . . . rather than having a wider view of what is best for the kids and community, it's down to a personal preference which is a pity.

The two primary schools that were part of the federation participated because the headteachers were particularly 'forward-thinking' and they had supportive governors (the chair of governors for secondary school is also chair of governors at one of the primary schools).

This short vignette has provided examples of how leaders have applied their *management intelligence* in the development of flexible structures and coordination of network routines within new and emerging structural arrangements. It has also highlighted the importance of combining social and leadership intelligence in order to develop and spread leadership within individual schools and across the network. It also highlights the importance of *contextual intelligence* in the early stages of developments, when individuals may be unclear as to the motives and rationale, or indeed the opportunities presented by adopting a collaborative approach.

The second vignette draws on the experiences of a city-wide initiative networking all 19 secondary schools in an attempt to raise standards across the local authority. The approach adopted intended to foster both school and systemic development at the same time. On the one hand, this experience provides insights into the potential for a coordinated networked approach across a city. On the other hand, the experience has revealed that the development of a system-wide strategy is far from easy, not least because of the presence of so many stakeholders, each with their own agendas and interests. It is here where we pull out the lessons for leadership in this context.

Vignette: social and contextual intelligences

A core purpose of this approach was to build leadership capacity. As part of this process, with the support of external consultants from IQEA, all of the schools created coordinating groups (school improvement groups or SIGs). Most of these consisted of colleagues with varied status and experience. Many of those involved in these groups were very committed to the work they undertook and grew in their skills and confidence developing their leadership and management intelligences as individuals within their schools and across the network. The active involvement of many of the headteachers and senior staff in working with the groups undoubtedly provided *contextual* and *social intelligence* supporting the capacity building processes. During the project some group coordinators gained promotion within their schools. This also contributed to the capacity building process and strengthened the profile of the network in some schools, confirming our experience that the development of leadership capacity within schools requires the active involvement of managers who are skilful in using processes of delegation in order to get things done. One of the challenges of developing a large network is the inherent variation in capacity across the network. Here we are struggling with cross-school as well as within school variations, a matter we shall return to in the final chapter. Therefore, in some schools, the contributions of the coordinating groups were limited, both within the school and across the network. The coordinating groups tended to make most contribution where their activities were seen as important, linking into school development priorities and not just as a bolted-on temporary project. The support and involvement of senior leadership within the school was an important factor contributing to the success of the coordinating groups. In some schools, too, the authority of the group would be helped by more active involvement of members of the senior leadership team and for some groups the realisation of previously promised meeting time during the school day would have aided their development, again highlighting the importance of senior leadership commitment in creating the conditions for collaborative and networking activity.

An important part of the initiative was bringing the coordinating groups together for workshops and residential events. With a network of this size, the tensions referred to earlier were very evident when it came to planning this type of programme, as were the different expectations of some of those involved. The residential workshops were in many ways remarkable, not least in respect to the large number of people who have been prepared to give their time, and to the buzz of energy and enthusiasm that has been generated. As with previous IQEA programmes, there were a series of dilemmas in designing a suitable programme. The schools were, inevitably, at different stages of development and, understandably, felt they needed for different types of inputs. Frankly, it seems unlikely such a programme could please all of the people all of the time. It was also clear that the most important part of these events was the debate and planning that goes on within the school groups in a context that offers space, time and climate for reflection. There was no doubt, too, that the IQEA team sometimes made the mistake of speaking for too long about issues that some group members viewed as being 'too theoretical'. Experience from previous projects suggested there would be a greater interest in such material and this may be explained by the nature of the schools and colleagues that were involved in those projects. A second explanation may be that the prevailing political context has led to an era that is dominated by a more instrumental climate. The after-school meetings presented similar dilemmas. Once again, however, they were well attended and have led to some splendid sharing of ideas, expertise and materials. As the initiative progressed, more was made of inputs from within the schools as a stimulus for discussion. The network particularly valued contributions from practitioners who come from other local authorities. Therefore, it would seem important that external consultants and network leaders adopt an outward looking perspective identifying what new knowledge and expertise can be brought into the network rather than becoming cocooned in the work of schools and the network itself.

Network events provided a context for sharing experiences and expertise between the schools. To some extent, this new emphasis may be a recognition of the dangers of placing too much emphasis on competition between schools as a means of motivating their improvement efforts. The work of IQEA has always involved school-to-school cooperation as a strategy for developing an inclusive approach to school improvement. These experiences lead to a strong belief that the idea of schools cooperating is the best way forward. However, most of this must be seen as an act of faith, since there is very little research evidence that demonstrates the extent to which such approaches can lead to positive outcomes, nor, indeed, evidence that can be used to guide action in the field. We hope that local authority-wide initiatives of this type will be able to gather more systematic evidence on the outcomes of such processes, as well as throwing light on the most effective means of achieving such outcomes. However, progress in this regard depends, to a large extent, on the quality of local leadership. This being the case, both local authorities and headteachers should be clear about the nature of new roles that headteachers need to take in sharing responsibility for the management of such collaborative arrangements. Headteachers have the challenging task of providing political and strategic leadership, both working with the local authority and also ensuring the network has the capacity for the day-to-day operational leadership within schools and across the network. This involves the headteachers working laterally with each other to provide strategic direction and ensure commitment from all schools irrespective of context or development phase, and also working vertically, within their schools but also with the local authority, working in partnership with or commissioning the local authority for services. While this has been the case for some time now, the challenges of establishing relationships within this context remain.

In this initiative senior officers within the education department demonstrated a commitment to a city-wide improvement strategy, involving all secondary schools, and working in partnership with members of the IQEA team. They also did a very important job in mapping how different strategies and agendas might be linked together in one coordinated strategy across the local authority. Meetings were held with members of the various advisory and support services to explore the implications of the developing strategy for their work. However, despite much effort, a good understanding of the emerging strategy tended to remain the preserve of individuals rather than the local authority. This had implications for the extent to which teams were able to rethink their roles in relation to school-led improvement activities. Once again, then, we are confronted by uncertainties and dilemmas that need to be debated and resolved. Here it is important to understand that the work of local authority staff is changing in relation to structures and relationships that have been fundamentally reformed over the last few years. These changes have been reflected most significantly in the evolving relationships between English schools and their local authority staff as a whole. In part, what we are aiming for, of course, is the strengthening of the partnerships within the local authority and between the local authority and schools in order to foster powerful interdependent relationships that add value to the work to all of the participating schools in developing a more equitable service for young people. This vignette illustrates the extent of the challenge, particularly in terms of redefining relationships and behaviours of those in key leadership positions, whether in schools or local authorities, and if we are to liberate the leadership capacity hidden within the system.

How do network leaders build leadership capacity within and across networks?

Recent research has highlighted tensions between the complex demands placed on school leaders and the ability of traditional models of leadership to provide solutions. However, the following study also identified early indications of how leadership practice was changing to respond to these challenges:

> It is unlikely that traditional patterns of leadership will prove adequate in the face of these new challenges. Accordingly, new structures and processes are necessary . . . There are increasing signs that leadership practices within schools are responding to these challenges.
>
> (Chapman *et al.*, 2008, pp. 4–5)

In situations where leadership practices are beginning to respond to some challenges presented by this complex picture through network approaches we see network leaders drawing on a number of key practices that build leadership capacity, including:

- *Demonstrating public support* – Senior leaders in positions of authority within the network are very public in their support for the network and individuals involved in the network. These strong words are also matched by actions. These leaders prioritise the network and provide resources to support networking activity.
- *Stretching leadership both within organisations and across the network* – Stretching leadership is a core process for building leadership capacity within the network. Network leaders invest time and energy in spotting, nurturing and releasing leadership potential within the network. They bring people together within and across schools. This coordination is deliberate and appropriately timed to maximise capacity building processes and ultimately the impact of the network.
- *Building cohesion at all levels* – Successful leaders manage the inevitable tension between organisational development and network development. They hold a realist perspective and draw on their 'intelligences' to identify when and where their efforts should be placed to build cohesion at all levels. These leaders ensure there is always an area within their organisation where networking activity can be shown to have a positive impact; this is also true for the network per se.
- *Promoting a culture of collaborative learning* – Successful leaders bring people together to learn from each other and reflect on their practices. These processes increase the social and intellectual capital of the network, improving relationships and generating and sharing new knowledge. Much of this activity focuses on the learning level and may involve activities such as lesson study, team teaching and action research projects.

- *Seizing opportunities to innovate* – Successful leaders tend to be opportunists and entrepreneurs and as network leaders are themselves personally well networked. They draw on their own networks, spotting opportunities and borrowing ideas, bringing them into the network. They are expert at linking ideas and initiatives to people within the network. This has the effect of bridging networks and building leadership capacity within the network. These leaders are also creative with resources and have the ability to subvert policy and the external environment for the network's benefit.

- *Paying attention to monitoring impact and outcomes* – Successful network leaders do not rely on their faith in networking, they ensure the network is data rich and the data are used effectively to inform decision making and to monitor outcomes. These leaders do not rely on one type or source of data, rather they draw on a range of data sources to evaluate a range of outcomes.

- *Looking beyond the network* – Successful leaders pay close attention to detail within the network but they also tend to be very outward looking and excellent horizon scanners. They spot shifts in the context early and adapt and respond very quickly ensuring the network is in the strongest position possible to exploit forthcoming opportunities.

What are the key challenges network leaders face?

While the above are key practices we see network leaders engaging in, building leadership capacity within networks remains a challenging proposition. The key challenges rise from the complexity of the job in hand. Network leaders face the challenge of dealing with a range of stakeholders, each holding different formal and informal roles and responsibilities within their organisation and the network, each used to operating within a set of guiding values/cultural norms within their organisation, all within an overarching context where organisations are expected on the one hand to collaborate with each other but on the other where they are set against each other in a quasi-market. Given this environment it would seem that network leadership and building leadership capacity are set to remain demanding and challenging aspects of school leadership for the foreseeable future. In an attempt to support network leaders through elements of this challenge we offer the following tool as a guiding framework or heuristic to consider dimensions of their practice.

Tool 4.1: mapping emerging patterns of leadership practice

This table provides some examples of emerging collaborative and networking practices within the English school system. The purpose of including this table is to provide a range of examples of emerging practice in some of the newest forms of school structures including academies, trusts and federations where collaboration and networking across organisational boundaries is becoming a common feature.

Table 4.1 Emerging patterns of leadership practice

	Within-school networking	Across-school networking	Beyond-school networking
Management	This school has a director of specialism (assistant head) who also leads on extended provision. Extended provision is staffed by non-teachers but gains educational direction from the director of specialism. The other assistant heads also manage support and curricular teams. Behaviour issues are dealt with by non-qualified teacher status (QTS) staff. In this academy the deployment of staff without qualified teacher status, notably the importance of its director of finance and the emergence of 'pastoral managers' from other professional backgrounds, is an important feature of its management structure. This all-through school is led by one principal who is supported by a senior leadership team of eight colleagues including two vice principals, and five assistant vice principals (AVPs). These are: one responsible for the business and enterprise specialism, one responsible for staffing and personnel	The senior management team in this federation has expanded to incorporate collaborative work with the primary feeder schools. There are 11 assistant headteachers all with specific responsibilities, both within and across schools; they operate a series of small sub-groups that focus on more particular issues. The impact of this restructuring is that less time is wasted and meetings can more effectively focus on specific issues. All schools involved in the federation and wider partnership have agreed a shared 'mission statement' founded on the eight conditions for raising student aspirations as defined by the GISA: 'we all want the same things'. This trust will become operational in 2009. In preparation the executive principal will redesign management structure. He intends to 'flatten' the structures across several schools. This may involve implementing a matrix structure, with leaders overseeing a specific phase but with cross-phase responsibilities e.g. the	In this school learning weekends now attract 450 local people each term and holiday schemes attract 70 per day. Wider collaborations are creating a coherent local offer, 0–19. Arts events and projects reach into feeder schools. At this trust the head and deputies have very different roles. In particular, it is very clear that the head is mainly preoccupied with taking the school forward, looking to outside partners to add to available resources. One teacher commented: '[The head] is more like a managing director … getting us known'. Meanwhile, the deputy head describes himself as a 'traditional deputy', focusing, in the main, on establishing firm and consistent arrangements to ensure that the school goes about its day-to-day business efficiently. This all-through school has been planned in response to the reorganisation of schools into the introduction of a two-tier system across the local authority. Here educators and the wider community

across 3–18, the two leaders of Key Stage 1 and Key Stage 2, and the AVP responsible for care and guidance. The establishment of a TLRI team of six was an important initiative to support the amalgamation. The appointees came from both primary and secondary backgrounds.

7–14 leader may have a whole-school responsibility for pedagogy.

are developing local solutions to meet the needs of the community.

Leadership

The headteacher at this trust invites new members of staff to spend an initial period getting to know the school and deciding how best they feel they can contribute. Such an approach contrasts with the more usual expectation that newcomers to a school will 'fit into the jigsaw' in a way that reflects the contributions of their predecessor. The Milburn approach to accountability tends to rely on a collective commitment to a set of values and the expectation that all members of staff will take a professional approach to their duties, doing their best for their students. With this in mind, some outstanding teachers are used as models of good practice – sources of inspiration for their colleagues.

This federation serves a large rural area of 300 square miles. The federation is perceived as the ideal solution to headteacher retention and threats of closure in isolated primary feeder schools. The headteacher of the secondary school and the chair of governors are viewed as the key motivators behind the development of a federation in this context: 'those two pioneers have now spread that initiative to all other primary feeders so next year they'll all be on board with it, its taken two or three years to get to that stage'. The headteacher of a primary school, one of the partner schools, is also seen as a key individual due to her enthusiastic and innovative attitude to the collaboration.

Supported by the local authority, the founding heads of this all-through school saw amalgamation as means to preserve education (3–18) for this community. There is now, however, a growing realisation that the 14–19 agenda is harder to achieve with a small secondary phase, therefore a wider range of networks are being developed.

The headteacher of this federation networks beyond the school and its partners. For example, under the threat of reorganisation he liaised with key players at local and national level to influence decisions relating to the future of the school.

Table 4.1 Continued

	Within-school networking	Across-school networking	Beyond-school networking
	The headteacher of this federation is frequently out of school. This provides space for the senior team to take on additional leadership roles. Temporary appointments to the senior leadership team also create significant professional development opportunities for middle-level leaders to expand their expertise and network with a wider range of colleagues.	Leadership in this academy has encouraged staff to work collaboratively with colleagues in the locality and to develop joint responsibility for the outcomes for young people across more than one institution or area.	The headteacher of this school is an influential and capable networker who has the ability to draw resources towards the school and community and influence key players at local and national levels.

External networking has benefited this trust school, local business sponsors have supported community programmes with financial backing, enabling vital outreach work to continue over many years. The schools also have excellent support from their local MP and councillor: 'without them we would have floundered'. They recognised early on the importance of networking beyond education to create a 'positive press' in the local community who can see 'we're a school making a difference'. |
| Governance | The governing body in this all-through school includes community, higher education and business representatives. It holds frequent away-day conferences to address important themes. Its members believe they are moving | This 3–16 school has a single governing body. It operates five sub-committees. The chairs of these form the important strategic committee.

This federation created a joint | When this academy was set up, the community was consulted about the mission. Now it is established, the governors' premises and community committee is seeking to engage with the community, facilitating and |

from passive receipt of information to active, informed support.

The governing body at this federation has been reduced from 23 to 13 and all committees have been abolished. Each member of the governing body has a specific responsibility (e.g. curriculum, estates, finance). The impacts of this change have been that the governing body works more effectively, members are better informed, more involved and more committed.

governing body to discuss common issues and make policy decisions. One governor, the headteacher and one other representative from each partner school sit on this strategic committee. Each school meanwhile retains its own governance and leadership. Under this arrangement, the partner schools also share some of their resources: each school puts £5 per pupil into a joint fund that pays for shared services, such as modern foreign languages expertise and library resources, a qualified librarian from Carromere College works in both the partner primary schools.

supporting access.

The sponsors of this trust, a university and a further education college, are highly regarded educational partners, both because they support the vision of lifelong learning and will assist the pupils in their educational journey. The key aim in this context of severe social and economic deprivation is the raising of aspirations in the local community. It has been recognised that pupils must be nurtured at every stage of their educational development, being particularly vulnerable at transitional stages, from three into adulthood.

Key for structural arrangements: ACADEMY   ALL-THROUGH SCHOOL   FEDERATION   MANAGED STRUCTURE   TRUST

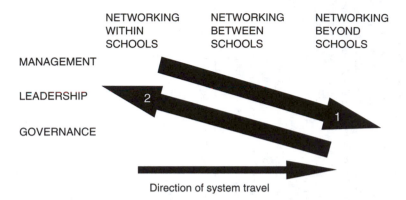

Figure 4.1 Network shifts in leadership, management and governance

The above tool is a heuristic designed to support school-based network leaders to reflect on their leadership, management and governance practices. It has been developed from research into new models of leadership which reported that leaders are increasingly being drawn into boundary activities working in partnerships and networks that span schools and other organisations. This is represented on the framework by the 'direction of system travel arrow' (Chapman *et al.* 2008) (see Figure 4.1). This tool can be used by individuals or groups to reflect on their networking practice within, between and beyond schools, and the implications for leadership, management and governance practice. The tool should be used in conjunction with the table describing examples of emerging practice in the field to consider potential opportunities for networking. The series of questions below are also offered as prompts and stimuli for discussion.

Issues for reflection

1 What demands does the network place on leadership, management and governance practice on (a) a day-to-day basis and (b) at a strategic level?
2 As a result of being part of the network what changes have been made to leadership, management and governance (a) within school, (b) between schools and (c) beyond school?
3 How have these changes impacted on others (a) within your school, (b) across the network and (c) beyond the network?
4 To what extent has being part of the network increased the leadership opportunities (a) within your school and (b) across the network?
5 What other measures have been taken to develop leadership capacity (a) within the school, (b) across the network and (c) beyond the network?

6 Which intelligences have been drawn on in order develop this leadership capacity?
7 How can we be sure the network is fulfilling its purpose? What evidence do we have to support this?
8 What opportunities are on the horizon?
9 How can these be used for the benefit of individuals and organisations within the network?
10 Who is not involved in the network activity but has the potential to make a significant contribution? How can the network secure their commitment?

The above issues for reflection are intended to locate shifts in practice that can be mapped out on the framework for exploring leadership, management and governance in networks and stimulate debate around important issues pertaining to leadership and the future development of the network.

Chapter 5

Sustaining and developing a network of schools

Introduction

It is a little unfortunate that this chapter comes so late on in this book as it could give the impression that sustainability is something only to be considered in the latter stages of building a network. In this chapter we try to counter this perception as we argue that the issue of sustainability needs to be both part of the initial strategic planning of any network and its on-going evaluation.

Why though have a separate chapter on sustainability? Surely if a network is well designed and well led its sustainability will take care of itself? The view we take is that the status of school networks, and the nature of networking, is such that unless consistently reviewed, their value reinforced, and adapted to meet new challenges and possibilities, then they will dissipate. This is primarily because the individual school still represents the basic, and default, organisational structure for the delivery of educational services in most localities. Even though the policy landscape in many countries may slowly be moving towards supporting various forms of collaboration, the legacies of earlier market- and competition-based policies still shape the context in which the majority of educationalists operate.

In addition, there are also specific sustainability issues faced by school networks that are worth considering in detail. Although networks can be both flexible and responsive, the structures and interactions that define them can also hinder their development. For example school networks can often suffer the effects of accretion. This occurs when a network's development is marked by the addition of new structure to support each new area of activity. If this goes on over a number of years then slowly the network starts to collapse under the weight of its own infrastructure. Similarly the managing and sequencing of differing interactions across several schools presents strategic coordination issues not normally faced within a single organisation.

What do we mean by sustainability?

When we apply the term 'sustainability' to a network of schools it raises questions about longevity and the demands it places on the resources of individual schools. Is it 'worth' the effort? What should be maintained? What should be stopped? This then leads on to questions about what actually helps a network sustain and be sustainable? Our own research into sustainable networking (Woods and Hadfield, 2006) and broader research that has considered the scaling up of educational reforms (Coburn, 2003) has led us to develop a framework for considering the main aspects of sustainability within networks of schools.

Coburn's (2003) review of reform initiatives within the US over the last two decades is particularly useful as she explores the linkages between sustainability and three key concepts: depth, spread and shift in reform ownership. Her argument, put simply, is that an initiative can be sustained in the face of competing demands if it has reached a critical mass of activity, scope, if it has done more that scratch the surface of schools' and practitioners' work, depth, and when it moves from being someone else's reform to being owned by those who are implementing it on the ground, shift in reform ownership. To identify the key aspects of sustainability we have incorporated Coburn's analysis of the scaling up of reforms with elements of network theory. This resulted in the identification of six key aspects which we have ordered to create our STICIT framework for assessing and developing the sustainability of a school network. The six aspects are:

- *Spatial*: the spread, and depth, of network activity.
- *Temporal*: the pattern of activity over time.
- *Interactional*: the nature and quality of the network processes.
- *Cultural*: the development of collaborative norms.
- *Infrastructural*: the nature of the structures within the network.
- *Teleological*: the purpose of the network and its inclusivity.

Spatial –The spatial aspects of sustainability are primarily concerned with the extent to which networking has spread across the schools in the network and also the depth to which it has reached within each school. Spread is important because it relates in part to the key idea of creating a critical mass of activity. Such a mass increases the likelihood of the networking being sustained as it can take on a life of its own separate from the cultures and agendas of the individual schools that contribute to it. Depth is key because unless networking eventually affects what happens in classrooms it will always be open to accusations of being peripheral to the main work of the school and so becomes an expensive luxury.

Temporal – The pattern of activity in a network can ebb and flow over time as it initiates and develops different activities. Monitoring and managing these ebbs and flows is important in ensuring that individual schools do not become overwhelmed by too much activity or are left out of the network activity for too long and so become distanced from it. Strategic leaders in successful networks identify opportunities to bring back in schools that have been dormant and disengaged, and recognise the need to let schools rest, or temporarily withdraw, when faced by losses of internal capacity or competing demands, such as an external inspection.

Interactional – The nature and quality of the interactions between members of the network, from the establishment of trust through to the development of learning relationships that allow for the effective transfer of knowledge and practice, are key. Assessing the quality of the processes that take place during these interactions and understanding how they may, and need to, progress is vital in ensuring the sustainability of the network. Just as important as the quality of individual interactions and processes is how these are sequenced in order to build capacity within the network and to ensure impact in the classroom.

Cultural – Developing a sense of identification with, and belonging to, a network is the starting point to mobilising effort and developing a shared sense of responsibility for its collaborative aims and objectives. Establishing these cultural norms are at the centre of the gradual shift within individuals, teams and schools from the network being perceived as an invention of others to something which is owned by its members. Cultivating beliefs and norms that support networking, and assessing how well networks have become established, are processes that underpin a network's sustainability.

Infrastructural – Every network needs structures to bring people together and help with the coordination and management of its activity. In terms of sustainability it is important to avoid developing a 'meetings' culture in which too much of the available resources within a network are spent on simply bringing people together to talk rather than working together. The structures need to provide sufficient flexibility to allow the network to respond to new challenges while not allowing the network to become fragmented. Similarly the structures need to be equally good at coordinating activities laterally, across groups and schools in the network, as they are vertically, between the different leadership and management structures within schools and the network itself.

Teleological (*telos*: end, purpose) – Last but not least is the issue of what the aims and intentions are behind all this networking, its overall purpose. Networks come together for all sorts of reasons from the altruistic to the instrumental, and so do the people within them. In the final analysis the core purposes of the network need to be sufficiently compelling to get and keep people involved and at the same time sufficiently inclusive to draw in a wide range of people. Maintaining the relevance of the network's activity to a wide range of schools and individuals, each at different stages of development, means not only evaluating current plans but also projecting forward the work of the network so that it meets the future needs of the schools and staff within it.

Building sustainability into the strategic plan of a network

Our argument is that for a network to be sustained, and to develop effectively, its leadership needs to build a consideration of these different aspects of sustainability into their process of strategic planning. In Chapter 2 we discussed how when initially planning the development of a network it was important to adopt a design process that flowed from purpose through to structure. Being strategic about sustainability requires those leading the network to turn this design flow from a one-off linear process into a continuous cyclical process where present activity is continuously reconsidered in relation to future plans. This cyclical process is vital to maintaining a flexible approach to the redesign of the network. Figure 5.1 tries to represent how issues of sustainability need to figure both in the evaluation of a network and its redesign.

The leaders of a network need to consider each aspect of the STICIT model as they move through different cycles of strategic planning and use them to review the sustainability of current activity and to plan the development of the network. As the leaders of the network move through these cycles they will be involved in three broad leadership activities, which we've termed the 'Three Es':

- evaluating what is and isn't working;
- embedding and growing effective network activities;
- evolving the network so it can take up new possibilities and deal with potential threats.

Effective network leadership will critically interpret the evaluations of what is currently happening and be prepared to act upon this analysis. Going forward

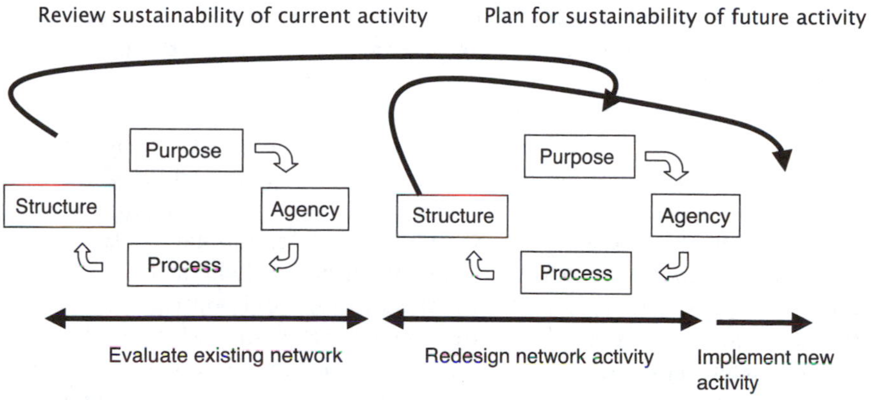

Figure 5.1 Planning strategically for network sustainability

they need to be able build the capacity to embed and grow network activity that has been shown to be effective and to carry out the adaptive changes required to take advantage of new possibilities and deal with emergent threats. Before we explore what is involved in each of these cycles by looking at the 'Three Es' in more detail we want to provide an overview of how the leadership of one network set about ensuring its sustainability.

Vignette: a light touch approach to sustainability

This collaborative grew out of a mini-education action zone (EAZ) and consisted of nine small primary schools serving the same inner city community. Both headteachers and teachers commented that they had found it difficult to take on board and assess the effectiveness of all the teaching and learning initiatives they had been introduced to when they were part of the EAZ. When the funding for the EAZ finished they decided to carry on working together, but decided they had to operate very differently now they were working with a much reduced budget and more limited resources.

The headteachers, who met relatively regularly, decided to form six smaller clusters of teachers each enquiring into different initiatives around learning and teaching that they had been introduced to when they were a mini-EAZ. (Their first strategic decisions therefore were to limit the number of processes, the learning and teaching initiatives, and to simplify their structure to reflect the fall off in funding.)

Within each cluster they decided that there would be three broad levels of involvement: 'lead' schools, which generally had more experience and more developed models of the learning and teaching initiative within the cluster; 'development' schools, which were committed to introducing or developing the clusters focus; and finally, 'watchers', which would simply be kept up-to-date with what was going on in the other schools in the cluster and would not at this stage be involved in any practical changes. This strategy of differential involvement resulted in each school being connected to all the various network initiatives but with each having a different combination of those they were leading on, developing or simply observing. The combinations that individual schools selected reflected their most pressing needs and current capacity. (The network leaders have tried to manage the ebb and flow of activity by allowing some schools with lower capacity to simply observe interventions while those with greater capacity were able to lead on more. They were also trying to ensure a greater depth of impact even if only with a restricted number of classrooms.)

Individual school leaders were able to match their collaborative efforts with their own school's situation. Headteachers focused only on those initiatives that they thought were suitable for their school at this time, while still learning about different approaches. The headteachers met the leaders of each cluster regularly and were able to assess the suitability of any new innovation for their own school, how it could be most effectively introduced and understand more about its impact and evaluation. (The headteachers had begun to evaluate the network more effectively by gaining a collective sense of how it was impacting on each of their schools. They were also developing a structure to ensure that the collaborative work of the clusters was linked to the development agenda of individual schools by regular meetings with the cluster leaders.)

Members of each cluster were able to call on those leading an initiative to work with them. They set up a range of mentoring relationships, planned and developed materials together, observed in each other's classrooms and even exchanged pupils so that those experienced in working in a new way could demonstrate it to pupils unfamiliar with an approach. (Here the infrastructure of the network was being developed to ensure that existing capacity was used to develop further capacity and ensure that the transfer of knowledge also resulted in the transfer of practice.)

Reviewing the sustainability of current network activity

In the first part of the strategic planning cycle the focus is on reviewing the sustainability of the network's current activities, and this involves its leaders in the first of the 'Three Es', evaluating what is and isn't working. A complete review of sustainability would be based on leaders evaluating all the network's achievements and current work against each aspect of the STICIT model. Such a review, as with any form of evaluation, would involve leaders in two broad types of activity, developing a better understanding of the network activities and achievements and making judgements against some form of criteria as to their quality or effectiveness. All evaluations vary in the degree to which they emphasise one or other of these activities and reviewing the sustainability of a network is no different.

Understandably, considering the complexity of the leadership challenges presented in the early stages of a network, the initial emphasis in most network reviews tends to be on leaders developing a better understanding of what is going on rather than a rush to judge its effectiveness. Establishing a collective understanding of a network's development amongst its leaders is a key part of the strategic planning process, and one that can be overlooked as they are often reluctant to admit a less than full understanding of what is going on. Because of the complexity of mapping back from any changes in classrooms to specific network activities, many leaders are also understandably hesitant about make overly simplistic judgements about how effectively their network has been. As such judgements are highly problematic it makes it all the more important that networks early on develop an evaluative culture that positively looks for the effects of collaboration and networking. Here one EAZ coordinator reflects on their view of the importance of developing the right evaluative culture:

> You have to develop the capacity to reflect on what the collaboration has done. Sometimes to spot the unexpected benefits and pitfalls that have

happened as well. These are ways of thinking you have to put in place before you begin. But there is a dynamic in most collaboratives that they have to be reflective in terms of what happened, to be able to identify what successes have come about, and maybe they weren't the successes that were intended. The ability to recognise the whole range of positives that have happened as a result of that collaboration.

(EAZ coordinator)

Reviewing network sustainability not only shares many of the character-istics, and problems, of any evaluation but it also involves additional com-plexities, the most significant of which is the multi-layered and multi-stranded nature of networks that bring together leaders, practitioners, students and different communities in a range of processes and structures. Differentiating between these levels and strands of activity and identifying 'network effects' can be simplified by focusing in on certain aspects of network activity.

To help leaders focus in we recommend that they use one, or a combination, of four broad 'lenses' through which various strands and layers of network activity can be tracked. These are:

• evaluation of network events;
• evaluation of networked processes;
• network-wide evaluations of shifts in views and perceptions;
• the network-based evaluations of school-based innovations.

Each of these four lenses can be reviewed using different aspects of the STICIT model to build up an evaluation matrix (see Table 5.1 in Tool 5.1). This kind of matrix can help leaders identify the best sources of evidence and existing data and where key gaps need to be filled by new evaluative activities.

Evaluation of network events

The vast majority of networks will carry out evaluations of major events, such as conferences and joint CPD activities. These evaluations generally focus on participants' perceptions of what happened during the event, rather than what arose from it, that is the actual impact it had within the classroom. The key issue here is that if carried out in isolation, event evaluations have little utility in assessing sustainability, but by repeating and targeting specific evaluations across a sequence of events they can track changes in the culture, reach and depth of impact, and provide leadership with a means of assessing network structures and processes.

There is no specifically 'networked' approach to event evaluation but it is important to keep in mind that when bringing people together from a variety of schools it might be useful to analyse how successfully it has met their needs on an organisational as well as individual level. This is because to be sustainable a network has to learn how to mediate between the network's focus and the developmental needs of individual schools, in other words to balance its purposes and aims with those of the schools who form it:

> We recognised that the learning and change that would take place might be different for each school depending on their context and the development of creativity within the curriculum at that time. We believed that it was important that the aims of the project and the nature of change could be facilitated within each of the existing school improvement programmes.
>
> (Network middle leaders)

A network is going to start to lose members if its events appeal generally to individuals but the needs of specific schools are not met.

Evaluation of networked processes

The major processes within a network will run across several events, could extend over months of activity and involve staff and pupils across a number of schools. For example network-wide action enquiry projects or curriculum innovations will by necessity involve numerous meetings and events at both network and school levels. Major processes will probably have their own specifically designed structures to support them and their own sets of aims and objectives against which their impact is to be evaluated. In some networks there might be several such key processes occurring at any one time.

The main leadership challenge here is to generate a holistic evaluation that not only encompasses the major strands of activity but also identifies the likeliest points of impact across different schools. As was discussed in the first chapter, the more focused the network intervention, the more noticeable and measurable the impact. If major network processes have been concentrated on a small group of practitioners or pupils then it is relatively simple to deal with by means of a targeted piece of evaluation. If several activities are on-going concurrently then networks have to build in a more systematic approach to evaluation.

As we have already discussed the first step in a more systematic approach to reviewing sustainability is to gain an overview of what is actually happening within a network. A useful starting point is to develop some kind of map of the network's structure and the processes. In Chapter 2 we provided some diagrammatic representations of network structures and in our own research within networks we have often tried to get network leaders to create some kind of organ-o-gram, which we termed a network-o-gram. The following diagram represents one network's views of its current structure (Figure 5.2).

This particular network-o-gram was developed as the network's leaders reviewed their work two years after they had started their network. The key change they were considering for the following year is indicated in the central column by 'pupils/students', and as it was in the planning stages, a question

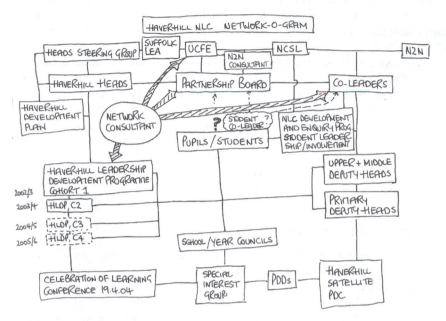

Figure 5.2 A network-o-gram
Source: Hadfield *et al.* (2004, p. 18)

mark. The proposed changes to the structure included the appointment of a student co-leader, bringing in school councils as part of the network's structure and creating a network pupil council. The process changes involved developing a stronger student participation and pupil voice aspect to the network and aligning this with the work of their leadership development programme, run externally by a local university. In the future, student participation would join leadership development as a high leverage activity focused on the two main aims of the network, improving the quality of learning and dealing with the transition issues between schools.

   Once the relationships between these major processes, old and new, and how they fit into the structure of the network are clear, then the task of evaluating their quality and impact becomes much easier. For example, coordinated school-based evaluations could focus in on the student voice work looking at transitions. These could then be collated, and backward mapped to network processes and structures, such as the special interest groups, the network pupil council and the work of the student co-leader, to assess their effectiveness. The techniques and tools for evaluating major network processes are no different from other forms of evaluations. The specific challenge for network leaders is in mapping them and their interactions and following the path from impacts through structures to the processes themselves.

The STICIT model can be applied equally as well to the sustainability of a specific process as it can to a whole network. So in the instance above the scope of the pupil voice work could be assessed, as well as the quality of the interactions between schools on either side of the transitions. The extent to which pupils 'buy in' to the network would also be an important indicator as to whether network-wide pupil voice activities are likely to be sustained.

Network-wide evaluations of shifts in views and perceptions

Networks of schools can appear very different depending on the perspective from which you view them. Some individuals and schools will be drawn in more rapidly to collaborative working than others, and this will generate very different views amongst leaders and participants on the network's effectiveness and impact. At certain points in the development of a network it can become important to create some form of a holistic overview of its development so its members can set their own experience within it and compare each other's, hence the popularity of carrying out surveys of participants' perceptions and experiences.

Surveys of participants can serve a number of purposes but they are particularly helpful in allowing the leaders of the network to grapple with the cultural aspects of sustainability, specifically the extent to which participants identify with the network and have developed a sense of ownership. Surveys are also a useful means of assessing the extent to which the network is meeting the individual and collective agendas of staff and pupils. For individual members feedback from surveys can help them understand the range of needs and interests present within the network and to what extent their experience has been the norm or an exception.

Network-wide questionnaire surveys are one of the commonest ways of creating these holistic overviews. They generally contain a range of questions from assessments of a network's current activities to participants' views of possible future directions. An example of this kind of survey was the annual 'Levels of Learning' survey provided to networks by the Networked Learning Group. This survey set out to assess the degree of collaborative practices and learning occurring across networks at a range of levels from pupils through to leaders, and to what extent they occurred across whole schools, between schools and at a whole network level. Although beneficial as a one-off these kinds of surveys are best when carried out on a regular basis, particularly because their analysis and feedback to strategic leaders is costly and can be complex.

Once surveys move on from trying to gain an overall picture of participants' views and involvement and try to help establish the impact of networking, they become a much more complex proposition. Not only does this require more detailed baselining, it also requires a more sophisticated form of questionnaire. To simplify the survey process networks often use pre-existing questionnaires rather than develop new ones and focus in on a very specific aspect of their potential impact rather than going for all-embracing surveys.

The difficulty that many networks face is that their developmental work is generally more sophisticated than their evaluative capacity so more often than not pre- and post-testing of new innovations is not carried out. This is why we have suggested an alternative approach in the next section that is based on a series of inter-visitations, interviews and observations as a means of assessing impact. Although more costly and more restricted in scale, this approach is much more likely to work with the evaluative capacity available within most networks, unless of course they have connections with an external evaluation team that has a solid foundation in designing questionnaires that look at impact. An additional benefit is that evaluations carried out by network members greatly assist the process of knowledge transfer.

Whether focused on creating a holistic account of a network's activity or trying to gain an insight into a specific area of impact, the value of these types of surveys is in leadership terms as much symbolic as it is practical. They gain their symbolic value by re-enforcing the identity of the network and individuals' membership of it, though to do this they need to be fed back to network members in an authentic and involving manner.

Network-based evaluations of school-based innovations

If the previous lens was very much about creating a macro overview, this final lens looks at network activity through the other end of the telescope. It considers how to evaluate a network's activity by focusing down on the impact it is having in a particular school or classroom. To an extent this occurs informally every time school leaders talk about what network activity is happening in their schools or whenever a member of a network working group visits another school to look at what they are doing. How though to formalise these processes so that they also contribute to the sustainability of the network?

A first step would be to increase the 'networked' nature of these processes by getting a range of network members to look at the work within a particular school. If such a group were then to visit more than one school they could start to compare and contrast how each school was utilising the input from the network and start to identify school- and network-based effects on what was occurring. Some networks have created a reference group of schools, a small sub-group of schools who were broadly representative of the network as a whole, and then focused a lot of their impact evaluation energies within this group rather than trying to prove impact across all the schools in the network. The inter-visitations themselves could also become more formalised so that the data were more systematically collected and evaluated and fed back to schools and the network as a whole. Such a systematic process of inter-visitations could then become part of the knowledge and practice transfer processes within a network rather than remain simply evaluative. One such approach to formalising the process of school-to-school inter-visitations is described in Tool 5.2.

Beyond making a direct contribution to the sustainability of the network, by supporting the transfer of knowledge and practice, such school-based evaluations provide one of the most powerful means of assessing the depth of network activity. This is particularly the case for those outside of the network who are less fascinated by the challenges of networking and collaboration and much more concerned about schools and classrooms.

Planning for sustainability of future activity

If leaders in the first part of the strategic planning cycle were mainly occupied with evaluating what was and wasn't working, in the second part of the cycle their emphasis switches to the second and third 'Es':

- embedding and growing effective network activities;
- evolving the network so it can take up new possibilities and deal with potential threats.

The key leadership challenges of embedding and growing existing network activity highlights concerns such as:

- how to achieve a critical mass of participants;
- how to get those participating in the network to feel they own it; and
- how to ensure the network activity impacts on classrooms.

These concerns place stress on two aspects of the STICIT model, the spatial and the cultural.

The spatial dimension of the model places emphasis on the spread and depth of participation. Spread is concerned with the lateral reach of activity within a network. By extending reach across schools and classrooms a 'critical mass' of network activity is more easily reached. Depth is concerned with the extent to which networking is not just for those who are involved in leading the network, but also has an impact in classrooms and affects pupils' learning and their lives: 'Depth means changing classroom practice, move beyond lip-service, getting into the fabric of the classroom, affecting the work with the children' (Network co-leader).

Achieving depth is about establishing network activity as an integral aspect of the life of a school rather than an add-on: 'Network activity needs to replace what is happening, not be put on top, needs to become a part of things, be bolted in not bolted on' (Network co-leader).

The cultural embedding that needs to occur to ensure ownership is linked to the spread and depth of participant. This is because the development of an increased sense of ownership of the network amongst headteachers, teachers and pupils results in part from a critical mass of practitioners translating network-based ideas and innovations into practice in their own classrooms. Once this occurs then they will no longer see it as someone else's creation or something that happens 'out there' and will recognise that people are not merely paying lip-service to the idea of working collaboratively:

If you are going to leave a legacy – something sustainable, you have got to change classroom practice – a lot of schools paying lip-service to innovations. In secondary, where schools are big, you have key people who are doing things, networking, and in reality that is where it stops . . . how much it feeds into teaching is negligible. It is getting it into the fabric of what happens in the classroom and change their approaches.

(Network co-leader)

If sufficient members of a network see it as their 'own' and feel both protective of and responsible for it, then, in the words of Cynthia Coburn, there has been a 'transfer of ownership'. Any reform is not 'at scale' until it has reached a critical mass and it is owned by those whom it affects:

[T]o be considered 'at scale', ownership over the reform must shift so that it is no longer an 'external' reform, controlled by a reformer, but rather becomes an 'internal' reform with authority for the reform held by districts, schools and teachers who have the capacity to sustain, spread and deepen reform principles themselves.

(Coburn, 2003, p. 2)

There are multiple leadership challenges involved in embedding networking activities into the fabric of classrooms across a network, but in terms of sustainability it is the skills of higher order capacity building (Hadfield *et al.*, 2002) that are key. In particular it is the leaders' ability to cohere and develop the collaborative capacity of their network. Collaborative capacity is what is required by individuals, teams and organisations so that they can work together and achieve their collective endeavours. It is also the capacity they need to be able to be adaptive and innovative, the final of our 'Es'.

Collaborative capacity in networks

The higher order capacity building required of network leaders is based on them developing and linking individual, team and organisational capacities for sustained interaction. Capacity building in this area is therefore both a professional developmental activity, improving individual and teams capacities, and a leadership activity, in terms of orchestrating and linking these into a viable and sustainable network. The added complexity of capacity building within a network is that there are multiple layers of 'internal' and 'external' capacities that need to be linked and developed. For example, a school will need to have a relatively high degree of internal capacity to interact with the external capacities that lie outside in the network. If teachers and pupils do not have the time, resources or skills necessary to interact effectively with others then there is no way they can access the external capacities of the network. Even if the network has a great deal of external capacity it will not 'stick' within a particular school unless it is aligned with their needs and the school has the capacity to absorb and use what is being offered by the network.

Network leaders will need to develop the skill of juggling and aligning capacities that can be highly dynamic over time and where there may be very variables rates of change. Certain parts of networks are more at risk of experiencing rapid changes in capacity than others. For example, smaller schools can quickly lose capacity, due to staff turnover having a greater proportional effect than in larger schools, and also gain capacity more quickly, as staff development and support will be easier to orchestrate in a primary school of ten staff than a secondary school of a hundred.

It is nigh on impossible to set out all the various collaborative capacities, individual, team or organisational, needed to sustain networking and inter-action. We have developed an outline model to help leaders consider what they need in their network (see Figure 5.3). The origins of this model are in our research into school capacity building (Hadfield et al., 2002) and it still shows its roots in the original work of Mitchell and Sackney (2000). The model is based on whole organisation, team and individual levels but these are split into both school and the network. Leaders have to harness, and align, this potential and focus it on issues of improvement, change and sustainability. To paraphrase Sergiovanni (2001) the different capacities of individuals and teams not only has to be developed and captured but also formalised and put to work if higher value assets are to be produced.

This outline model can be applied to any network, but we have completed it with reference to a relatively well-established network that is looking to extend its work locally. Hence the key leadership challenge at a whole network level is to influence the external context in ways that shape it to become more conducive to networking. This would see the network leaders working as 'system leaders' creating the external conditions for collaboration. At the school level the key leadership challenge, in terms of building collaborative capacity, is maintaining the connection between the individual agenda of schools and the overarching purpose and aim of the network.

As an outline model of collaborative capacity we have highlighted the kinds of leadership, structures, norms and practices that need to be present and set out the range of groups and individuals to be worked with. Higher order capacity building involves the leaders developing these separate elements but also cohering them at different levels. What though do leaders need to do to develop and cohere these various capacities? They need to do the very same things that will also ensure that the network is able to meet new challenges and explore possibilities; that is they need to develop an adaptive form of leadership that can deal with both the internal dynamics of the network and the changing contexts in which they work.

Adaptive leadership is defined by a number of characteristics:

* the ability to diagnose, mediate and coordinate the needs of different groups (Barge, 1996; Hersey et al., 2001, Day et al., 2000);

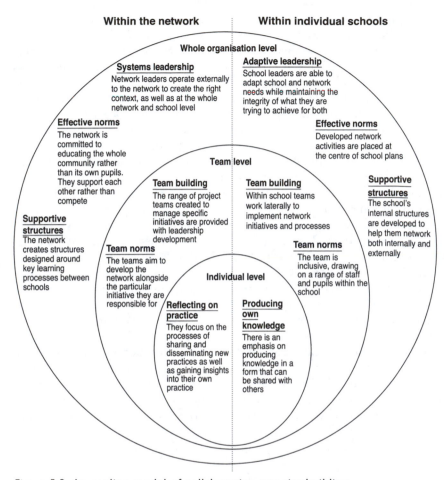

Figure 5.3 An outline model of collaborative capacity building

- sufficient sensitivity to deal with the paradoxes and complexities of their work while retaining their integrity (Woods and Woods, 2004);
- a commitment to developing and sustaining the leadership of others who can also act as adaptive leaders (Hargreaves and Fink, 2004);
- the skills necessary to move others beyond their personal and organisational interests so that they consider broader learning and social welfare goals (Woods and Woods, 2004).

Ultimately leaders within the network need to be able to develop this form of leadership not only amongst themselves but also across the different teams and groups they are working with.

Guidance for network leaders about reviewing activity and planning for the future sustainability of the network

Evaluating what is and isn't working	What balance do you want to strike between developing a better understanding of what is going on and making judgements about its effectiveness?
	There are four key 'lenses' through which network activity can be reviewed, these are: • Evaluation of network events. • Evaluation of networked processes. • Network-wide evaluations of shifts in views and perceptions. • The network-based evaluations of school-based innovations.
Embedding and growing effective network activity	To be sustainable a network has to learn how to mediate between the network's focus and the developmental needs of individual schools.
	Embedding existing network activity is based on creating a 'critical mass' of network activity by expanding the network's reach across schools and by ensuring it has real depth of impact into classrooms.
	The key aims culturally are to get people to own network activities and build identification with the network.
	Embedding networking into the fabric of classrooms requires the building of collaborative capacity at all levels of a network. This is the capacity of individuals, teams and organisations to work together and harness their agency so it can be applied to their collective endeavours.
Evolving the network	Building collaborative capacity is based on developing and linking individual, team and organisational capacities for sustained interaction. Capacity building in this area is both a professional developmental and leadership activity.
	Leaders within the network have to harness, and align, this capacity by finding answers to the following questions: • What connections need to be made between schools and teams to link the collaborative capacity we already have and what form should these linkages take? • What types of connections work best between what areas? • What kind of strategy is needed to guide how and when these connections should be made? • When do certain connections need to be broken and replaced by others?

Tool 5.1: developing a strategy for evaluating the sustainability of a network

There are four steps to developing an overarching evaluation strategy that focuses on the sustainability of a network.

Stage one

You need to have developed a 'map' of the network that shows its key structures, groups and processes by creating a network-o-gram or similar overarching description. Details of how to do this are given in the tools section of Chapter 3.

Stage two

Identify the evaluative activities that are already in place and what they are focused on by indicating on this map where you are currently carrying out evaluations of

- network events;
- networked processes;
- network-wide shifts in views and perceptions;
- school-based innovations.

Stage three

Now decide on which aspects of the STICIT model you want to consider in the evaluation. You can use the 'Aspects of sustainability' framework (Figure 5.4) to generate the evaluative questions you wish to consider in each area of the model. Be clear about the extent to which you are interested in understanding what is going on and how concerned you are with assessing impact.

Stage four

You should now use the 'Evaluation matrix for sustainability' table (see Table 5.1) to identify the data you already have and what extra information you want to collect in order to develop your understanding of the particular aspects of the STICIT model you are interested in. You now have to decide on how best to collect this information.

Cultural

How widely recognised is the work of the network, by whom? How much is establishing trust an issue? What, if anything, has generated a lack or trust? How much has joint activity resulted in shared beliefs? To what extent is there a sense of this being 'their' network, the teachers and pupils, rather than 'yours', the school leaders? What do schools find difficult to share with one another? To what extent have practitioners developed a shared sense of responsibility for learning across the network rather than just in their school?

Temporal

Have you noticed a rhythm and flow to network activity? How important is it that the volume and scale of activity increases? Has the level of activity reached a plateau in some schools and in some processes? Have you noticed any natural/key increments in growth of network activity?

Spatial

How wide is the reach of the network? Are any schools becoming disconnected? How deep is the work of the network? What areas have been easier than others to achieve reach and depth? Why? What have been the areas that have failed to percolate into classrooms? Should they be continued?

Aspects of sustainability

Interactions

What range of interaction is currently taking place? What is being learned in these and what processes do you see as having the greatest value, and for whom? What difference are these key processes making? What is the impact in the classroom, on pupil learning? Who is not engaging, why? Are the interactions between staff properly sequenced so they result in classroom change? What things should you stop doing now, next year or in the near future?

Teleological

To what extent are current processes and structures developing and directing the kind of capacity you need? What demands on your current capacity do your future plans make? To what extent do you plan for reach and depth of involvement? How inclusive is that planning across and within network schools?

Structural

Have you got the right balance between processes and structures (the flight path)? What strategy is in place to ensure that schools and staff are given the opportunity to participate in network activity? Is there a structural aspect that describes how that strategy enacts itself? To what extent is the strategic planning made explicit in action? What structures are created to underpin strategic plans?

Figure 5.4 Aspects of sustainability

Table 5.1 Evaluation matrix for sustainability

	Spatial	Temporal	Interactional	Cultural	Infrastructural	Teleological
Evaluation of network events						
Evaluation of networked processes						
Network-wide evaluations of shifts in views and perceptions						
Network-based evaluations of school-based innovations						

Tool 5.2: network inter-visitations – a network-based approach to evaluating school-based innovation

Network inter-visitations are a process that focuses on the impact of a particular aspect of network activity within specific schools or classrooms. An inter-visitation programme within a network can play a range of roles in the development of a network or a specific school-based innovation.

Different types of inter-visitations

Baselining and building mutual understanding – At the beginning of a network's life inter-visitations often focus on the general context of schools within a network. They help to create a baseline of current activities and help in the identification of good practice and areas requiring further work. These inter-visitations require a tight focus but the framework used is not overly judgemental, rather it simply tries to build up a comparative picture across different schools. These types of inter-visitations require network members to visit multiple schools to build up an overall and agreed picture. These visits basically build up a series of snapshots of current work.

Understanding the development of good practice – Once a network has built up a baseline picture, the next stage is to focus in on good practice that could be exchanged and to assess any areas of concern. Here inter-visitations may focus upon the 'lead' school within a network or they can also be used diagnostically to look at areas of weakness and concern within a certain school or the whole network. The data collection framework shown later (Figure 5.6) was used to help those involved in an inter-visitation build up a picture of how an example of good practice had developed over time. Such frameworks need to be developmental, not only focusing on current good practice but also how it has come about over time. Several visits by different groups may be required to understand how good practice has come about.

Monitoring of an innovation – This final type of inter-visitation concentrates on the implementation of a new initiative. Here a series of visits has to be planned in advance so the implementation can be monitored as it proceeds. The data collection framework used has to be able to identify any problems, highlight successes and account for both to those involved in leading the initiative.

What follows are three sets of materials to help you think about how you can develop your own programme of inter-visitations:

- a sequenced overview of the process (see Figure 5.5);
- an example of a data collection framework (see Figure 5.6);
- an outline plan of a school visit (see Table 5.2).

An overview of the inter-visitation process

An inter-visitation programme has a number of key stages. The first stage is to identify its focus. Focusing in on a specific aspect of network activity requires you to go through a selection process. This process needs to be based on discussions within the school and the network. The next stage is to think about what you are looking for that could indicate a 'network' impact. This impact might be on a range of areas and so you need to be clear what these are and what you are going to focus on. This list of potential areas of impact, from the leadership of the school to specific changes in classroom practice, becomes the start of the data collection framework you will use to look for evidence that network activity is having an impact on the school you are visiting. Next you need to use this framework to create a list of questions you want to ask or things you want to look for on the visit. The next stage is the actual visit itself, which needs careful coordination. After the visit it is important to provide feedback to the school and consider how the process could have been improved.

Stage one: Defining a focus for the inter-visitations

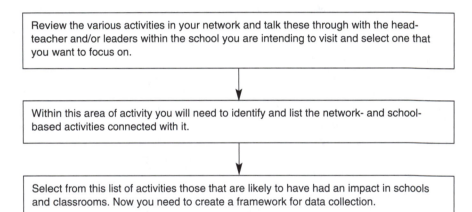

> Review the various activities in your network and talk these through with the head-teacher and/or leaders within the school you are intending to visit and select one that you want to focus on.

> Within this area of activity you will need to identify and list the network- and school-based activities connected with it.

> Select from this list of activities those that are likely to have had an impact in schools and classrooms. Now you need to create a framework for data collection.

Stage two: Developing a data collection framework

> The first step in creating a data collection framework is to generate a list of key questions you want to ask about the activity you are focusing in on. There is an example of one such framework on the following pages and it consists of a series of sub-questions under each key question (see Figure 5.6).

Figure 5.5 A sequenced overview of the process

The next step is to decide how you will answer these questions, through collecting evidence of impact by observing in classrooms, looking at documents, reviewing pupils' work and talking to staff and pupils.

You may want to collect evidence of impact from several sources and at various levels from changes to teachers' knowledge and practices, through how pupils' learning is being affected, to its impact on pupils' levels of attainment.

At the level(s) you have decided to collect your data you need to create tools for collecting and recording evidence of impact. These might include interview guides, observation sheets etc.

The next stage is to turn this series of tools and sources into a schedule for a visit.

Stage three: Planning and carrying out the visit

Now you need to plan your visit by deciding on who in the visiting team is going to talk to whom, about what, to build up the evidence to fill in your data collection framework (see following outline plan for a visit – Table 5.2).

Check the plan through with the school to be visited and clarify expectations with the teachers being observed or interviewed. Obtain all necessary permissions for recording or photography within the school.

Carrying out the visit will involve making observations in the classroom, interview pupils, staff and leaders. You need to build in time not only to collect the evidence you need to assess impact but also to carry out ongoing analyses. This could involve you in discussing your interpretations of pupils' work, school documentation, photographs of the environment and what you drew from the interviews.

Figure 5.5 Continued

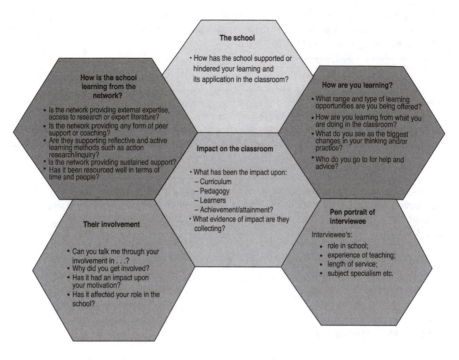

Figure 5.6 An example of a data collection framework

Table 5.2 An outline plan of a school visit

Stages	Evaluative reflections on the process	Issues/actions
Preparation for the visit: • Agree focus • Create framework • Agree list of questions • Identify participants • Arrange schedule for visit	Did we have an agreed understanding of the process? What were the expectations of each person in the visiting team? Did we have the right people in the team?	
Classroom observations Pupil questions: • What are you learning? • Why are you learning this? • How can you get help with your work?	What were we looking for when we visited classrooms? How much time was needed for this to work well? What should we have done differently? Who should lead this process?	

Table 5.2 Continued

Stages	Evaluative reflections on the process	Issues/actions
Staff/leaders interviews: Use questions from the data collection framework (Figure 5.6).	Did we give sufficient time for this? How well did the questions work?	
Debrief After visiting a classroom, participants share what they saw and heard and relate this to the focus of the visit. Coordinator of the visit invites each participant to pose a thought-provoking question or make a non-judgemental comment that would prompt the thinking and learning of the leaders and teachers about the next steps to support pupil learning.	Were the visitors prepared adequately to feed back on what they had seen in the classroom they had visited? Do we need an agreed pro forma to do this? Did we agree any next steps? Who is responsible for them?	

Chapter 6

Working the net

The role of the external facilitator

Introduction

The need for some form of external facilitation of networks is one of the most common findings within the early research on networks of schools. What is less clear is what these facilitators actually do and why they are seen as so important. You could develop a sneaking suspicion on reading some of the early research that as many of these accounts of university–school networks are often written up by the university staff that facilitated them that 'they would say that wouldn't they?' In our own research (Day and Hadfield, 2004; Chapman, 2006), we have also argued the case for an individual, or group, external to the network having a role in its strategic development. In this chapter we are not going to spend a great deal of time defining the notion of facilitation; rather we are going to concentrate on the potential benefits of having a facilitation capacity that is external to a network.

The chapter breaks down into three broad areas. First we discuss generally what is meant by external facilitation and delve into some of the debates around how it differs from leadership, who should do it and how the role needs to develop with the network. The next section looks in much more detail at the types of roles that external facilitators take on from critical friends to brokerage. This section tries to give a flavour of the range of skills and aptitudes needed by those involved in facilitating without trying to define, or favour, any particular 'model'. Finally we look at the broad strategies used by facilitators in networks to engage both leaders and practitioners.

So what do we mean when we talk about 'externally facilitating' a network of schools?

A lot of the confusion around the idea of facilitation within networks arises not so much because of the range of definitions that exists, or even how such a role relates to or differs from being a consultant, mentor or coach, but because people consistently misconstrue what is meant by 'external', or even overlook the word altogether. In practical terms leaders at all levels of a network will take on aspects of a facilitator's role. That is they will be working across a range of relationships where their primary agenda is to help those involved work together and learn from each other. The basic role of the facilitator in a network is not really that different from those who work with a single group or on one-off events; it is essentially to ensure that people participate fully and gain what they need from the group or event.

Facilitating participation and engagement is particularly important in networks of schools because they often involve the establishment of new relationships across institutional boundaries and between cultures that have not only kept people separated but also at times placed them into competitive or antagonistic relationships. We used the following quote from Madeleine Church at the very beginning of the book but we wanted to repeat it here to remind the reader of the centrality of participation in networks, and because it aptly sets out the job description of what the facilitation capacity within a network has to do. That is to effectively 'work the net' to ensure the right forms, quality and scope of participation:

> Participation is at the core of what makes a network different from other organizational or process forms. Who participates (issues around power, and resources), how they participate (issues about relationships, coordination, facilitation, governance) why they participate (issues around vision, values, needs, benefits, motivation, commitment), and for how long (issues around sustainability).
>
> (Church *et al.*, 2002, p. 14)

So central to the role of anyone facilitating a network is the issue of participation. They care for the 'net' by looking after the relationships and interactions that form it, and they work the 'net' so that the network functions effectively. This means that they have to deal with the issues around power and resources so that there is a degree of equity in who participates. They need to look at how people participate and support relationship building and aid better communication and coordination within the network. They also need to help participants reflect on and articulate why they are involved, or should get involved, in network activities. To do all of this they need to understand aspects of group dynamics, how to build trust and consensus and how to understand equality issues. All issues in fact we have already covered when discussing how the leaders in networks need to work. So if there is no apparent difference in the agendas, skills and understanding required by network leaders and what we might call network facilitators, why introduce the term at all? Well because once you link it to the term 'external' then we are talking about individuals who will bring a 'little something extra' to a network, which can have a powerful impact upon it. This little something extra is generally one of three things:

- a perspective not available to those within the network;
- a position of being both inside and outside of the network;
- an enhanced external ability to connect to external resources.

Let's unpack each of these ideas in turn and consider how they might play out with respect to the different roles taken by external facilitators.

First of all let's consider the issue of perspective and what it means to be 'external'. In many ways this is a nonsensical piece of terminology because by their very nature networks have fuzzy and elastic boundaries, so in what sense is anyone who engages with a network outside or external to it? At its simplest the term simply denotes that the facilitator is not based within one of the network organisations, a position we shall discuss later that has a number of advantages. But in terms of having an external perspective facilitators may come from a different professional background, hold a particular theoretical viewpoint or have an area of practical expertise, and each of these can be an important addition to the leadership mix.

One of the first school network coordinators we came across was an ex-bank manager who, as part of his redundancy package, had opted to take on a voluntary job with a group of 30-odd primary schools in an inner city community. Using his business skills he negotiated a number of new contracts with the local energy and book suppliers so that the schools saved money and then went on to negotiate a series of funded projects with a range of organisations. For example, the local police service ran a safety campaign across all 30 schools rather than having to negotiate with them all individually. Now you may think this is stretching the idea of being an external facilitator a little, but the brokerage and negotiation skills he needed to draw all the headteachers into these contracts and projects were considerable and the savings made and extra funding created helped them to pay for a series of collaborative professional development events. This coordinator brought a business perspective and background in contract negotiation that added considerably to the collaborative of 30 schools and started to move them towards becoming a network.

The power of an external perspective is more than the simple addition of expertise. It should represent a challenge to the naturally occurring 'group think' that tends to develop amongst the leaders of a network. An external facilitator will challenge the way a network is currently working by presenting its leaders with alternative forms of collaborative working and different potential futures. We have worked with school improvement networks where our ideas about the role of research and enquiry in developing teaching and learning constituted a dramatically different perspective on how to define and identify effective classroom practice and share it across schools than was present at the time. We basically set out an agenda around improvement based on school-based initiatives rather than relying on externally imposed curricula and pedagogy.

A particularly powerful form of external perspective held by an external facilitator develops when they do not work constantly within a network but instead have a more 'punctiform' relationship. This is one marked by a pattern of regular intense activity with the network separated by periods of relatively limited contact. This pattern requires the facilitator to reconnect with the development of the network between visits, and in doing so get its members to discuss how they ended up where they are now from where they were the last time they worked with them. This process is naturally evaluative as network members unpack and articulate their view of the story to date. The external perspective here is one that might be called a 'critical friend'. The external facilitator builds up a close relationship through the various visits but the gaps between them gives the facilitator a critical distance, while the re-construction of the narrative of the network amongst its members helps them understand their own involvement and development.

Second, an external facilitator sits in a unique position within a network being at one and the same time an insider and an outsider. The key point here is that they do not 'live' within any of the organisations that form the network. They therefore do not sit within their leadership and management structures, they do not draw their status and rewards from them, neither are they 'normed out' by their cultures and beliefs. This gives the facilitator an independence of thought and action that are important to a network. This is because the facilitator should have the capacity to model risk taking and counter cultural behaviour within the network, while operating flexibly and responsively outside of the bureaucratic systems of individual schools. If deployed effectively by network leaders these two capacities can help deal with the numerous conflicts of interests that occur, help overcome some of the inevitable resistance to working in different ways, and challenge the innate conservatism that exists within most educational systems.

The network facilitator also has some choice in how they position themselves as 'insiders', which can give them a degree of flexibility when working within the network. They can position themselves as being impartial 'insiders' in that their focus is on the working of the network as a whole, not an individual school, a position that most school-based senior leaders cannot, in all fairness, adopt. The facilitator can therefore place themselves at the centre of a common tension, between the needs of individual schools and the network as a whole. By doing this they can help avoid this tension corroding the relationships between school leaders while they work on resolving the issues that has given rise to it. As they have a degree of flexibility they can also at times become 'advocates' of a particular approach, process or set of beliefs that the network has become involved in or previously espoused. As an advocate they can draw attention to and remind leaders and participants of earlier commitments, prevent the network drifting into simply chasing funding and so keep it focused, and they can also help ensure that its actions and activities are in keeping with its stated aims and values.

The final affordance an external facilitator brings to a network is that they often work and operate in a wide range of organisations and have extensive professional contacts, and can connect these with the networks they are facilitating. They are ideally placed to bring in these external organisations as they have an insiders' perspective on the network and can bridge the cultural, administrative and professional barriers that often limit a network's ability to draw down such external capacity. A good example of this from our own research was the considerable difficulties school networks faced within the NLC programme of connecting effectively with local universities to support them. A requirement of the application process for funding was that networks in this programme had to show how they expected to link with the existing knowledge base in the area of work they were involved in. Although this requirement was interpreted in a variety of ways, many networks sought to connect with a local university to draw down some form of research or enquiry expertise. From research carried out on behalf of the programme (Campbell *et al.*, 2005) what was clear was that connecting with an appropriate person within a university who was able to offer appropriate support was a relatively hit and miss affair, and was most effective when it was brokered by someone from within the network.

In summary what distinguishes the contribution of the external facilitator from 'internal' facilitators is that they are external to but well connected with the network. They can bring a perspective or expertise missing from the network as they have the potential to stand outside of the needs and desires of the individual organisations that form the network and so can focus on caring for and working the net. In such a role they can position themselves as being neutral or an advocate as they challenge insiders' ideas about how the network has and should develop. They are also ideally placed to lever in additional help through their connections with other organisations.

The role of the external facilitator: from critical friends to brokers

The range of titles given to external network facilitators gives a sense of the different aspects that constitute their role. In the networks we have researched they have been termed critical friends, consultants, brokers, coaches, change agents and strategic advisors. The combination of roles an external facilitator actually takes on is dependent upon the maturity of the network, what patterns of participation have already been established, the nature of the major processes they are supporting and the scale and level they are operating at. In the following vignette we discuss our own involvement in externally facilitating a network of schools and try to illustrate how it was shaped by these factors.

Vignette: facilitating a new network from initiation to implementation

This network of 12 primary schools arose from the concerns of a single local authority education officer who had responsibility for a group of schools that were marked by high pupil mobility combined with high teacher turnover. These issues when combined with changes of leadership had put considerable 'stress' on the local school system. Alongside these contextual problems she was also concerned that many schools and teachers had become dependent on 'outside' intervention to solve their problems as a consequence of responding over many years to the imperatives of a centrally driven curriculum and the assessment agendas of successive governments. She felt that there was a need to support the development of teachers through engaging them in research into their practice that would create new knowledge about teaching and learning. It was this desire that led her to approach a local university team to become external facilitators of the network she wanted to form.

The network initially started with the academics using their previous experience of supporting action research and networks to set out a basic set of aims, processes and structures to groups of headteachers and senior teachers in each school. The suggested process was school-based action research that would be facilitated by the academics. In each school a SIG would be formed that would include teachers and learning support assistants. The SIGs had responsibility for the day-to-day running of the action research projects, which were the major collaborative learning processes within the network. The SIGs were constructed so as to build internal capacity and to ensure that dispersed leadership was practised from the outset. So each group was led by a SIG coordinator who was any member of staff other than the headteacher, and membership was voluntary and inclusive to try and encourage as wide a range of staff involvement as possible. In some of the smaller schools the whole staff elected to be part of the SIG. A timetable of regular, monthly meetings for SIG coordinators was facilitated by local education authority and university staff. These meetings were a forum for establishing and sustaining collaborative working processes, addressing issues arising from the action research projects, providing training, giving each other mutual support and also passing on information about individual projects. The meetings started with just the SIG coordinators attending but increasingly they were attended by at least one other member of each SIG as a co-leader, thus addressing the issue of succession planning.

At the start of the project, through a process of internal and external facilitation by university and school-based staff, a series of classroom- and school-based analyses and self-evaluation processes were set in progress that helped schools decide on an area for research. Individual schools selected foci that were particularly relevant to their own context: these included areas of the curriculum such as assessment, developing thinking skills, inclusion and gifted and talented pupils. The range of foci raised concerns about how they would be supported but this was balanced by the need to build trust in the network and to develop ownership within schools. The university staff set up a series of workshops and events around carrying out action research and as the network progressed relationships formed, particularly where schools had a similar research focus. Individuals also kept in contact outside the meetings through telephone calls, emails and occasional visits to each other's schools.

As the network developed the role of the external facilitators started to change from developing the action research processes to working more with the strategy group of headteachers that oversaw the network. This group met each term and was composed of headteachers and the local authority officer who acted as the network coordinator and internal facilitator. One of the first issues that arose was that as the SIG coordinators developed confidence in their roles, they wanted to have their leadership 'on the ground' represented in the strategy group as they felt that the headteachers were often out of contact with the pace of their work. As the university team worked with both groups, it brokered the expansion of the strategy group to include a SIG coordinator.

As the action processes process evolved so did its facilitation, which quickly began to focus in on helping share its outcomes and transfer knowledge around the network. One way of doing this was to launch a series of annual 'milestone' conferences. These conferences acted as a means of sharing and celebrating the progress of individual school action research projects and also evaluating progress and considering new areas for development in the following year. The facilitation processes here were about looking for overlapping and common issues so that schools started to recognise and work on shared problems rather 12 separate projects. This began to fundamentally change the network's perception of itself and influenced the strategic decision making processes.

The external facilitation team also set out to explicitly remind the network leaders that they needed to reconsider how they should be used as they re-contracted with them annually. In the first year the emphasis was on supporting the network leaders getting things going. In the second year it was more explicitly about capacity building, supporting SIG coordinators to train up additional staff in action research, planning for succession, getting the network to take more ownership of the milestone event. During the second year, as the leadership became more comfortable with the idea of being in a network, the role of the external facilitation team began to shift again. Although still being used to support action research, particularly with the new schools that were joining, they also began to work more on the boundaries of the network looking at how to attract additional external funding and for ideas that could stimulate further innovation.

As external facilitators the university staff worked at several levels in the network and across several major processes. In terms of action research they acted as critical friends, processes consultants, led seminars and training events, and offered individual SIG coordinators technical advice and moral and emotional support. With regards to the leadership and the strategic decision making they tried to ensure equitable leadership and open decision making structures that would give the network credibility. They also worked with the internal facilitator, the local authority officer, to ensure that the leadership did not become over dependent upon them and actively considered how they should be deployed.

In the previous vignette we tried to illustrate the various roles competent external facilitators might take on if they have both generic facilitation skills as well as expertise within a specific area. When we were developing our roles within this particular network we also had had some experience of working in other collaboratives that made it easier for us to decide how to work. The level of prior knowledge of networks an external facilitator has can be an important factor in who you choose to work with and how you end up working with them. If as a leader of a network you simply want them to provide generic facilitation support, say, to a single group of senior leaders, then it is a less important requirement for them to have an understanding of networks, but if they are going to work across different levels of the network it becomes much more important.

Selecting and contracting with an external facilitator is not easy. Network leaders are often limited in the range of people they reach out to and they can fail to make a clear distinction between getting someone to coordinate the network and someone to facilitate it. This lack of clarity about the role when combined with a limited choice of candidates can result in very expensive external facilitators doing basic administration and administrators being pulled into rather complex facilitation roles. Our advice to network leaders in this situation is threefold. First, sort out the coordination and administration of the network: meetings do need setting up, minutes taken and finances managed, all of which can be time-consuming and, if done poorly, very destructive of new networks. Second, when building a strategic leadership team take advantage of any 'free' external facilitation on offer but use this initially to help you identify the gaps in your internal capacity and to define the role you would like any external facilitators to take. By 'free' we mean that networks of schools often have a wide pool of external contacts who might work with them for a few hours or days on a voluntary basis, at least initially, but would not want to take on a longer term commitment. Third, once you are clear about the type and range of external facilitation you require then consider how you will manage your relationship over time, and how you will use it to develop your internal capacity for facilitation. Too often networks don't develop their own capacity or fail to renegotiate the role of the external, or even change the external, so over time they increasingly fail to meet their changing needs.

Working strategically as an external facilitator

So far then we have considered the particular benefits of having an 'external' facilitator and the range of roles they might take on at different levels within a network. In this section we now move on to consider differing overall approaches to external facilitation and start to consider how these may be more or less appropriate considering the particular stage of development a network is at. Here we want to emphasise the idea of facilitating 'a network', not just a meeting or a single group within a network but trying to work holistically and strategically across it.

Our own research into how local authority and school district personnel were working within and across networks in their areas (Chapman *et al.*, 2004) is our starting point for the following analysis of the strategic approaches used by external facilitators in supporting networks. What we found was that their strategies changed quite dramatically depending upon their understanding of networks, the maturity of the networks they were working with and the extent to which school networks and networking more generally had become an established way of working in their area. We want to discuss these strategies in some detail because the majority of research that exists tends to look at more specialised or limited examples of facilitation. This means that currently the role played by facilitators in the strategic development of networks is little understood but new and immature networks often reach out to external facilitators for this kind of help. Leaders of new networks therefore need to be particularly aware of the pitfalls, as well as the positives, in getting in external support.

We identified three broad approaches to strategic facilitation in our research depending upon whether the external facilitators focused on the structures, processes or individuals within networks. Within each of these three broad foci we set the specific strategies used by the facilitators along a series of dimensions:

- a focus on network structures: from architects to landscapers;
- a focus on network processes: from knowledge creators to knowledge replicators;
- a focus on network agency: from brokers to animateurs.

A focus on network structures: from architects to landscapers

Although we would always argue that structures are not the best starting point for designing a network, getting them right is important and, particularly early on in the life of a network, getting them wrong has the potential to do real harm.

Network architects

This approach tended to be used by facilitators working with new or emergent networks in authorities where networking was relatively new. Facilitators who acted as network architects were often instrumental in deciding upon the composition of the schools that were to join the network and focused on helping its leadership design what they saw as an effective leadership and management structure. They tended therefore to be concerned about network coverage in the area; that is ensuring all schools had access to a network and joined the 'right ones' and that the various school leaders who were being brought together would operate well as a group.

As they were often working with a blank canvas with relatively few strong school networks already existing and because of the concerns they had about coverage, they tended to work in a less voluntaristic fashion than other facilitators. Not only getting involved in who should be in the network, they also focused on creating a simple leadership and management structure to which they as the architect would be relatively central. So, for example, they would suggest a single leadership group made up of all the headteachers, each of whom would appoint a person from their school management team to coordinate the day-to-day work of the network. The strategic leadership would meet once a term while the coordinators group would meet more regularly. The external facilitator would be the only person who was part of both groups and would support each in developing their roles.

The simplicity of this leadership and management structure placed the facilitator in a position where they could monitor the development of the new network, and while supporting both strategic leaders and operational managers they could also manage tensions and issues that arose within and between them. Such a leadership structure would also mean that the network was more accessible to those from outside who wished to connect with it, an important issue in a locality if a number of new networks were being developed at the same time and coordination between them was an issue.

This approach worked well when the architects increased the credibility and effectiveness of the leadership in the network by ensuring an equitable spread of power and authority throughout the network. This meant developing the initial leadership structures so that they fostered active participation by a range of stakeholders in the network, leading to a broadening commitment to the network. This approach worked less well when facilitators under-played the importance of building schools' commitment to opting in to the network and over-played the need for clarity and simplicity, failing to recognise the 'messy' nature of most networks. In these situations schools could feel forced or co-opted into networks they didn't want to belong to due to a fear of missing out on either new ideas or funding.

Being an 'architect' tended to be more popular with network facilitators who worked in authorities that had only recently decided to develop networks, and who had not applied the idea of a more networked education system to their own ways of working. In these instances problems could arise if the need to develop networks quickly combined with a desire for simplicity resulted in network structures and compositions based more on fitting in with the authorities' own bureaucratic structures than the preferences and interests of local schools.

Network landscapers

This approach was adopted when the external facilitator was working in a context where there were a number of mature networks. It was based around getting existing networks to adapt their structures so that they allowed for more network-to-network interaction and so that they were more responsive to what was occurring locally, rather than acting as autonomous groupings. Facilitators who acted as landscapers tended to work in organisations that had already restructured and re-cultured their provision into more networked structures and individuals tended to be more comfortable with the complex and messy nature of networking.

As landscapers they worked strategically with network leaders to consider how their network needed to develop so that it would work in harmony with the local context. The emphasis of their advice therefore tended to be on the link between the network and its environment with the facilitators acting as what Crandall *et al.* (NLG, 2005) describe as a 'boundary spanner':

> While we found that many of the leadership roles in networks were internally focused, our research also suggested the need for a leader to link the network with the external environment. The boundary spanner buffered the network by dealing with outside constituents, shielding the network from external 'noise' in the policy environment and by monitoring change in the external environment (e.g. new policies and regulations).
>
> (NLG, 2005, p. 29)

The difference being that in Crandall's case the stance of the boundary spanner appears essentially defensive, buffering the network from the effects of the local context. In contrast the network landscaper was proactively trying to engage networks with their locality, particularly other networks and the authorities' own networked services. This was primarily done by trying to align leadership structures so that network leaders from across the authority would meet, and linking the authorities' local services into individual network structures.

These external facilitators gained credibility because their own organisations were modelling a more networked approach themselves:

> We have adopted an approach that models the principles that we are trying to get schools to adopt. Therefore we have begun by creating a networked

authority by creating an infrastructure that promotes networking as a modus operandi. Now that schools are seeing how we work and the benefits associated with it they are beginning to configure themselves into networks.

(Local authority officer quoted in Chapman *et al.*, 2004)

A focus on network processes: from knowledge creators to knowledge replicators

Networks of schools come together for a variety of purposes, from the political to the financial, and this influences the types of processes its members engage in when brought together. As we have already discussed there are two main types of processes in school networks. There are coordination processes, which are concerned with leadership and management, and generative processes that create new capacities within the network. Although there are various forms of generative process, most are concerned with professional development of some form or with knowledge generation and the transfer of practice. Network facilitators who focused in on processes adopted a strategy of bringing these two sets of processes together in order to build greater coherence and connectivity.

Knowledge creators

The strategy of these facilitators was based on using enquiry process to explore possible 'network' solutions to key issues that they posed to the strategic leadership. The enquiry process was underpinned by the joint definition of issues and questions between the facilitator and the leadership of the network: 'Posing questions and collecting information from a variety of sources and perspectives is central to our approach and we use it to challenge our assumptions and instincts' (Local authority officer quoted in Chapman *et al.*, 2004).

This strategy required a degree of familiarity with enquiry by the facilitator, a willingness within the leadership to engage with it, and a capacity within the network to carry it out. The approach had utility for both new and established network where existing enquiry practices could be adapted to exploring possible responses to new initiatives and insights.

The facilitator's role was to coordinate the enquiry process with the decision making processes of the strategic leadership. This meant ensuring that the right forms of strategic questions were being asked by the leadership so that an enquiry process could be initiated across the network schools. The facilitator then had to shape these questions so that they were relevant at different levels in the network and coordinate the enquiry process so that it fed back in time to the strategic leadership of the network.

This approach was adopted by external facilitators when faced with networks that were already established but wanted to move forward into a new area or where there was a lack of agreement about the future direction of the network. It was also used by these local authority networks as a means of getting networks to consider what their stance would be to new local or government policies. Rather than trying to impose these new initiatives or policies on networks, their central aims or consequences for schools were put forward as enquiry questions, an approach that network leaders found much less threatening.

Knowledge replicators

Acting as a knowledge broker and being involved in the transfer of practice and understanding across a network is a widely recognised aspect of an external facilitator's role. It became a much broader strategy when the strategic development of the network becomes based on the identification of innovative or good practice, either within or external to the network, and its replication across the network as a whole. Facilitators who enacted this strategy not only helped in the identification of the practice but also advised on how the networks' own learning and leadership structures needed to be developed and linked.

The replication of good practice across a network might be a case of them taking on more widely an existing improvement in one of the network schools, or adopting a more collaborative or networked form of an external initiative. In some instances it might involve linking one network with another and transferring practice between them: 'This project has enabled us to reflect on the success within our local authority and build on our early gains by sharing best practice between networks as well as launching new ones' (Local authority officer quoted in Chapman *et al.*, 2004).

This was a popular strategy in localities where there was an uneven development of networking. This meant knowledge about networking and networking structures were well developed in some areas but only emergent in others. The facilitators used the more developed networks as not only sources of good practice ideas but also for their expertise about networking itself: 'We are developing a toolkit and have identified key experienced network leaders who are being asked to support the development of new networks in the authority' (Local authority officer quoted in Chapman *et al.*, 2004).

The key issues here were how good practice was defined and by whom. In most cases facilitators were honest brokers supporting network leaders engaging with the current knowledge base around new innovations and helping them consider the evidence of what 'works'. In other cases though it was clear that as local authority officers they wanted networks to engage with new initiatives and they were prepared to use their position as facilitators to develop this engagement. It wasn't uncommon for facilitators to select a network school to be one of the pilot schools for a new policy, a move frequently appreciated by the school and network as it would often bring in extra funding and resources. They could then use this pilot school as a demonstration school within the network knowing that other schools would be more responsive to learning from one of their own schools rather than one outside of the network, and they could also make use of the network's existing processes for transferring practice.

A focus on network agency: from brokers to animateurs

To an extent the facilitation of any network inevitably involves working on the agency of key individuals and groups, so all those we researched saw this as part of their role. This concern with individual or collective agency became a defining strategy when facilitators were working in a network where this is either an inherent tension or conflict or where there is a systemic lack of capacity. What kinds of networks are these?

Although it is hard to think of networks, which are voluntary and collaborative, as having inherent tensions or conflicts, they do exist. A classic tension inherent to mixed networks of small primary and large secondary schools is that not only are there likely to be major differences in institutional needs and agendas between these groups, but also their speed of reaction, their capacity to innovate and their resource bases are all affected by difference in size and scale. Similarly networks in inner cities can suffer systemic problems with capacity due to staff turnover and more frequent external inspection. Facilitating networks in these often dynamic contexts is as much a reactive challenge as it is a proactive one.

Focusing on the agency of individuals, groups and schools was to a degree a deficit strategy based on dealing with a fundamental problem with the network, which if not addressed would either lead to it breaking down or its development being halted. This was an approach that required the facilitator to have a strong insider perspective of the network they were working with and the confidence of its leaders.

Brokers

Facilitators acting as brokers were common in networks where a number of powerful well-established school leaders had conflicting or divergent views about issues such as the needs of the other schools in the network, how the network should operate in its locality, or its future direction. Here, the credibility and inter-personal skills of an external facilitator were viewed as a key lever in moving the network forward: 'We find it very useful to have experienced colleagues from outside to work directly with the networks. They provide a level of objectivity and facilitation that it is hard for us to deliver' (Network leader quoted in Chapman *et al.*, 2004).

It became a strategy when such competing agendas were recognised not just as a temporary conflict of interests but as inherent to the composition and nature of the network. Operating as a broker meant the facilitator would either try to deal with these tensions themselves or draw in another individual from 'outside' the network. In locations where other networks were operating successfully they would often draw on their internal facilitation capacity and ask them to moderate the group of leaders or try and rebuild some form of consensus.

Brokering in an external moderator could have a number of advantages for these local authority-based facilitators because of the micro politics of their local contexts. Generally they could position themselves as being neutral over most issues around the strategic direction of the network but as local authority officers they could be positioned as having an agenda beyond that of the network. If the conflict within the network was around an area of local authority policy they would lose the flexibility of neutrality. Brokering in someone else to deal with the tension or conflict could restore this sense of neutrality while re-enforcing the network's perception that it was refocusing its own work rather than being driven by external factors.

Brokerage is a complex role and draws the facilitator into the centre of the micro politics of networking. It requires skills of mediation and consensus building and relies upon them positioning themselves within the strategic leadership team so they can deal with the conflict within it. Although not unheard of in voluntary networks of schools, particularly when changes of senior leaders in schools upset established relationships, this strategy was more likely to be found in networks that had been 'put together' either by requirements of a funding source the network schools wished to access or by the local authorities themselves.

During the time this research was being carried out it was apparent that this kind of brokerage was also increasingly being required to deal with conflicts between different networks as it was within network tensions. These tensions arose because increasing numbers of schools belonged to more than one network. This could mean one network could find different combinations of its schools in a variety of other networks. Such multiple membership not only had the potential to create cliques and sub-groups within a network but could also put schools under considerable strain to meet various networking commitments. Mediating between a patina of networks was a situation many of the local authority facilitators had become very familiar with.

Animateurs

If brokerage was about dealing with almost an excess of agency, or at least conflicts between powerful individuals, and schools becoming involved in too many networks, facilitators who became animateurs were facing the opposite situation. This strategy was adopted when it was necessary to reinvigorate and re-engage leaders with networks that had lost momentum: 'Our key challenge is to improve the level of engagement of a few of our networks and to support the regeneration of some that have lost a bit of momentum' (Local authority officer quoted in Chapman et al., 2004).

In these situations the facilitators found themselves faced with a lack of engagement by school leaders in the strategic planning of a network and a gradual disengagement with networking by their staff. Here the challenges were to draw school leaders back into discussions about the network's overall aims and vision and to re-engage staff with network activity.

There might be numerous reasons why schools had become disengaged, to do with internal factors as well as the network itself. The first steps in re-engaging school leaders was to set up some form of consultation process across the network, which often required the facilitators to improve existing channels of communication and to create more imaginative approaches to decision making rather than relying on a series of meetings. Making communication easier and decision making more dynamic were all part of overcoming the 'busy' culture of schools that tended to make them inward looking and unwilling to engage in discussion of key issues: 'If the communication channels were better and the structures were in place then we would be able to consult more deeply on the important issues . . . but we are all busy and it is very difficult' (Local authority officer quoted in Chapman et al., 2004).

Effective animateurs once they re-engaged headteachers and senior leaders moved on to other tiers within the network. Here the main issues were about ensuring that someone was responsible in each school for overseeing effective connections with the network and that network activities were well led. Some animateurs set up leadership development programmes for these individuals while others provided informal mentoring and support.

Although in the original research these different approaches to facilitation were described as 'strategies', because at the time they encapsulated the issues and tactics that dominated what the facilitators were doing, they could also be viewed as different aspects of working strategically as a network facilitator. They fit well with the key aspects of network design. Dealing with issues around purpose and agency were very much the concern of the brokers and animateurs, while processes were the focus of knowledge creators and replicators, with architects and landscapes working through the redesign of network structures. Combining these approaches together provides us with a model of strategic facilitation (see Figure 6.1).

This model is useful to network leaders considering hiring an external facilitator to work strategically across their network. It can help them match the areas they need support with and the type of expertise they are looking for. Working strategically across a network requires facilitators to have expert knowledge of the aspect of networking they are supporting and in-depth understanding of the network.

When considering whether to involve an external facilitator network leaders have to consider the added value they bring, whether it be a specific expertise, an independent viewpoint or additional contacts and access to the existing knowledge base. The role they play and how this develops over time, especially with regard to the internal capacity of the network, has to be built into the initial negotiations. When external facilitators are being asked to work at a strategic level, across a whole network, it is important to match up their areas of expertise with the needs of a network.

Figure 6.1
A model of facilitating strategic
elements of a network

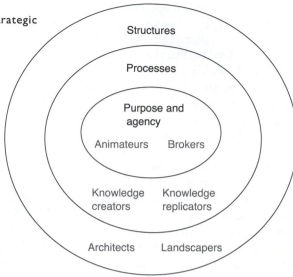

Guidance for network leaders about the use of external facilitators in developing
their network

What sort of 'external' facilitator do you need?	Do you require general facilitation capacity or more specialist external help that can support you in developing some of the major process and structures within your network?
	External facilitators with generic skills and a good understanding of the facilitation process can help you with issues about participation in groups and meetings. You will need someone with knowledge of how networks operate to help you deal with broader network-wide issues around participation.
	What bit of being 'external' will add most value to your network: a general outsider's perspective, specialist knowledge, someone with experience of other networks, an independent thinker or links to external expertise and knowledge?
How could you best use them?	How are you going to balance and coordinate your internal facilitation capacity with the work of your external facilitator?
	At what levels does the facilitator need to work? Is it primarily within one level or do they need to work across all levels so they can link developments?
	What form of whole network facilitation strategy would best suit your network at this time? Should it concentrate on individuals and the relationships between them, does it need to focus on the key learning process you use, or are the network structures right?

How should their role evolve?	What aspects of the facilitator's role could eventually be handed over to network personnel? What should they be doing after the first year? After the second and third years?
	What are the core issues and processes the facilitator is best placed to deal with? How could they support you in developing your internal facilitation capacity?
	What pattern of working with the network would best fit within its rhythm of activity and development? How can you keep the facilitator connected with the network?

Where do we need our external facilitator to work?

Good external facilitators who have knowledge of networks are a limited and often expensive resource. Network leaders therefore need to be clear about which of the most important areas they should focus this resource upon. The following tool (Tool 6.1) is designed to help senior leaders consider this issue. It is based on a framework drawn from our own research, Chapman *et al.* (2004), into school improvement within inner city schools. This framework consists of seven key levers for change:

- generating positive relationships;
- focusing on teaching and learning;
- distributing leadership;
- committing to continuing professional development;
- building community;
- creating an information-rich environment;
- exploiting external support.

Working collaboratively in a network should help every school in the network 'pull' these levers and therefore change the internal conditions of the school and the way staff work.

The tool asks you to consider how well your network is helping your school ensure each lever is in place. The idea is that the facilitator's work should be focused in on those areas that are working less well than others. The tool is in three parts and the first explains the framework by defining the levers and gives examples of how an external facilitator could support their usage. The second part of the tool consists of two case studies of school networks whose worked is reviewed through this framework. Finally a blank pro forma is provided to help network leaders record their views on what key areas an external facilitator should work on.

Tool 6.1

Part one: a framework for determining the focus of an external facilitator

Table 6.1 The focus of an external facilitator

Key lever	Definition of the key lever	Possible external facilitator input
Generating positive relationships	Involvement in a network should help build trust: encouraging people to be open with each other and take risks. Without this a school's capacity is limited as teachers are less likely to share, develop ideas and practice.	External networking helps staff gain confidence in their own work and become used to explaining it to others. It can generate more internal networking as staff find renewed interest in the work of their colleagues.
Focusing on teaching and learning	If the network is focused on teaching and learning this helps ensure school-based professional development and change improving what and how pupils learn. When a network concentrates on a specific area of teaching and learning it translates into immediate benefits in the classroom.	Expert external facilitators may already have developed their own curriculum improvement or reform package or be able to build a more bespoke approach for a specific network. They can help identify and validate existing good practice in the network and support its transfer and exchange.
Distributing leadership	An effective network gives staff the opportunity to take on new leadership roles. It provides them with new responsibilities, both within their school and with other schools. Staff may be asked to lead on an innovation, a cross-network team or a particular part of network activity. It exposes them to different leadership approaches.	Facilitators with an expertise in leadership can be involved in mentoring new leaders or may evolve a network-based leadership development programme. More generalist facilitators will work alongside such leaders in the development teams or SIG they are leading.

Committing to continuing professional development	A network should offer a greater quality and range of formal and informal professional development opportunities than can be offered by a single school. These may range from opportunities for enquiry into existing practices to transferring innovations that have been tried and tested elsewhere. The network should support the consequent process of change and embedding of new practices.	An external facilitator should help build the school's capacity to run its own professional development. To do this they may well work across very different levels from the strategic leadership to supporting less experienced staff designing and running CPD activities in conjunction with more experienced staff in other schools.
Building community	Networks help build a sense of headteachers and teachers as part of a wider community of learners and should develop a broader sense of responsibility to educating the community as a whole. This should reduce competition between schools and cliques within them.	The emphasis of the facilitator is on building new sets of relationships between headteachers and teachers outside of one's own school and normal reference group. This requires the building of social and professional bridges.
Creating an information-rich environment	The network should provide greater collective expertise in the use of different forms of data to help improve pupil achievement. Data and data gathering processes should be shared between schools.	Facilitators will work with leaders and teachers to view the use of data as an interactive and on-going process of collecting, analysing, monitoring and evaluating the impact of changes of classroom practice on pupils.
Exploiting external support	The network should provide a cost-effective means of drawing on expertise from external experts, i.e. higher education institutions and independent consultants. It should also be able to provide guidance and advice on who to work with and how to work with them.	The facilitator should help broker in the external expertise. This might involve them in identifying and contracting with external experts. They also need to ensure that external inputs are available in a form which can be used by individual schools on an on-going basis.

Part two: two case studies

Case study of a feeder school network

In this network the six primary schools and one secondary school have been involved in various forms of networking since they came together as a 'feeder' school network eight years ago. This network is based on a range of groups such as coordinators of gifted and talented and newly qualified teachers. These groups are involved in a range of action research and enquiry projects. The schools share a catchment area marked by high levels of socio-economic deprivation. The secondary school is a large urban comprehensive with pupils achieving poor results compared to the local average and poorer still compared to the national average. The secondary school has experienced significant change since it achieved specialist college status in 2002 and has increased its intake due to the closure of a neighbouring school.

Case study of a secondary school improvement network

This network made up of six secondary schools has worked together for nearly four years supported by local authority funding and working within a well-established school improvement programme coordinated by a local university. It has recently attracted additional funding to continue its work. Although the funding levels are reduced, they do not require them to follow a specific improvement programme. The network contains two schools challenged by low attainment and above average levels of pupils with SEN. Neither school was able to reach the average level of attainment within their local education authority or nationally.

Table 6.2 A feeder school network

Levers for improvement	What the facilitator can use to 'work the net'	What are the issues they need to address?
Generating positive relationships	The feeder primary schools have long-standing collaborative relationships. They have a range of cross-school steering groups that coordinate different strands of networking activity – for example, joint INSET (in-service education and training) and headteacher inter-school visits. They also belong to multiple other networks (gifted and talented, beacon, for example) that compete for time. The strong relationships between schools have developed groups of teachers who are comfortable looking to colleagues outside their school for solutions to problems.	Although a good level of trust has been established between the headteachers and some deputies within the primary schools there is more even development between them and the secondary school leadership. At present one of the major issues is whether the relationships amongst network leaders are strong enough for them to deal openly and critically with the competing demands of the different groups of practitioner researchers and enquirers.
Focusing on teaching and learning	There are already active groups focusing on reducing learning loss experienced by gifted and talented pupils as they move from primary to secondary school. This focus has brought the primary and secondary schools together under a shared agenda. Some of the primary schools are also working on reducing early years learning loss. The data generated from the enquires has the potential to feed into professional development on teaching and learning.	With transition conceptualised as the movement between primary and secondary as well as Key Stages 1 and 2, it limits the number of teachers who can be involved in the network. How can other teachers be brought into the network and how can their findings be made more relevant to all teachers in the network?
Distributing leadership	The network is providing opportunities to generate leadership capacity below the headteacher level. The cross-school research group is responsible for leading classroom-level improvement. Historically NQTs have also lacked development opportunities and they are now responsible for leading school improvement through their enquiry. Network leadership is also distributed across several schools. For example, four headteachers run the steering group.	The middle leaders in the secondary schools may be less successful as the opportunity to effect whole-school or even departmental change is limited by the sheer size of the institution. These middle leaders need more time to effect change and support. The sheer range of network working groups can result in a lack of coordination with too many disconnected meetings. With only four headteachers on the steering group, those schools who are not represented may lose opportunities to participate.

Table 6.2 Continued

Levers for improvement	What the facilitator can use to 'work the net'	What are the issues they need to address?
Committing to continuing professional development	This network is committed to enquiry-based learning. A local higher education institution created a bespoke enquiry training programme to fill a gap in their staff's skill base. This rolling programme involving 10–12 staff a year is generating a critical mass of teachers skilled in enquiry able to sustain it in the future. Through involvement in enquiry groups, school staff are moving into a state of informed professionalism.	The facilitator needs to develop the network leaders' understanding of the problems and possibilities of networked enquiry. With six primary schools and one secondary school in the network, primary teachers will be in a majority in the initial cohorts. This imbalance will make joint primary–secondary enquiries less likely.
Building community	There is a very flexible and inclusive approach to the nature of network involvement within each school. Schools can tap into network resources in a way that meets their individual needs. Teachers can more easily find others across the network with similar foci to work together in groups with shared interest.	Although individual flexibility has brought schools into the network it may create a situation where schools prioritise their immediate needs making networking a question of solely personal advantage instead of collective gain. The facilitator needs to look at how to move the leadership on from the short-term needs of individual school to a consideration of the gains that could be reaped through long-term network involvement.
Creating an information-rich environment	The network has created a number of enquiry groups that are developing teachers who are 'data-smart'. These are teachers skilled in evaluation and the use of evidence. They also become increasing self-critical and reflective as they grow more comfortable with receiving and giving feedback.	Little effort is being made to coordinate enquiries across the network to generate insights with a wider use. Unless the network builds on earlier work and activity elsewhere in the network, enquiry may simply become a series of fragmented projects rather than an accumulation of knowledge and deepening of understanding.
Exploiting external support	The network has formed an on-going relationship with a local university to provide support for enquiry. Individual schools find that external input shifts their thinking and develops deeper understanding.	The network initially only saw the university as a training provider rather than a strategic partner with which it could develop a more sustainable relationship. The facilitator needs to develop a more expansive reciprocal relationship with the local university and to identify other relevant external resources.

Table 6.3 A secondary school improvement network

Levers for improvement	What the facilitator can use to 'work the net'	What are the issues they need to address?
Generating positive relationships	These schools are a largely homogeneous group with a history of working together through a range of initiatives that were more or less collaborative such as IQEA and Excellence in Cities. The network has developed incrementally over a number of years moving from hosting groups that functioned as tips 'n' tricks swap shops to a network with established practices of collaborative enquiry.	The gradual development of the network does not place stress on schools through sudden leaps in demands. But this long history may lead schools to relax into 'cosy' and comfortable collaboration rather than cutting-edge or challenging learning relationships. The facilitators may need to bring new and more challenging approaches to collaboration.
Focusing on teaching and learning	The teachers are collaborating around six themes of cross-school work. The diversity of network activity means that individual schools should be able to find at least one aspect they find interesting. This inclusive model has enabled buy-in and provided a sense of momentum in the network.	The six themes can diffuse effort at the expense of gains that could be made through joint work in a smaller number of initiatives. The themes demand considerable coordination to ensure groups do not 'trip' over each other and it takes time to build up in school groups who are interested in each area. Now the network is operating with much reduced funding the facilitator needs to support the network leadership in considering how sustainable their current approach is and whether it needs to be modified.
Distributing leadership	Strategic direction and network overview is provided by a steering group of six co-leaders (one for each theme) and six headteachers. Each co-leader leads a theme group in which theme champions from all levels who lead developments in their respective schools meet weekly. Theme activity is integrated with school improvement plans.	In this complex structure, the headteachers find it difficult to stay on top of it all on a day-to-day basis and they require help with their strategic planning. The quality of co-leaders is crucial – they must be highly enthusiastic, strong and skilled in coordinating leadership development and mentoring. The facilitator needs to support those currently in post and to develop some form of succession planning.

Table 6.3 Continued

Levers for improvement	What the facilitator can use to 'work the net'	What are the issues they need to address?
Committing to continuing professional development	In addition to school improvement theme groups, all staff are involved in twilight sessions, residentials, end of year celebratory conferences and whole-school INSET with places available to staff in other schools.	The facilitator needs to help network leaders recognise that currently the range of activities places a high demand and requires a substantial time commitment from those leading individual themes. Equally schools at times feel overstretched and can buy into too much and not meet their stated aims.
Building community	A climate of trust, familiarity and openness with practice is founded in a long-shared history of cross-school working. The network's size means that at least two schools are involved in every activity. With a bedrock of demonstrated commitment, the network is comfortable with levels of involvement from full engagement to shadowing and watching.	The range of levels at which schools can participate may result in some schools becoming peripheral for considerable periods of time. The rhythm of participants' involvement in networking needs to be monitored and managed.
Creating an information-rich environment	Enquiry activity supported by a paid external researcher. Theme champions trained in techniques to interpret and use data. Standardised approaches to enquiry are employed across schools.	The employment of an external researcher does not build internal capacity and could create dependency. External researchers may be too detached from the network to understand its needs.
Exploiting external support	Existing link with partner from school improvement consultancy built into their strategic planning. This partner has good prior knowledge and understanding of context. Brings best practice research scholarships (BPRS) into network. One school is a 'super-networker' involved in a range of networks and initiatives.	Strengths • The 'super-networker' accesses resources and develops skills of those in lower capacity or less experienced schools. • BPRS builds research capacity of schools. • Making the school improvement consultant a partner creates 'inside-outside' capacity. Weaknesses • Failure to look outside for other external partners as too funnelled through existing expert.

Chapter 7

Where next?

Introduction

In this chapter we want to draw together the key concepts around networks and collaboratives and discuss how they relate to emergent policies and issues within education systems in the UK and internationally. In doing so we want to not only provide insights into the potential future for more 'networked' education systems but also the nature of the leadership such systems will require. Of course we are not alone in attempting to do this. In what was the first sustained consideration of the potential of networks in education, the OECD (2003) came up with a series of future scenarios. These varied in the extent to which networks became the norm and to the extent they operated as part of an education system or in fact became the system. One scenario, which they called 'learning networks and the network society', encapsulates their view of what might be the case if education systems were not organised by bureaucratic or markets means and instead became 'fully' networked:

> Dissatisfaction with institutionalized provision and expression given to diversified demand would lead to the abandonment of schools in favour of a multitude of learning networks, quickened by the possibilities afforded by powerful, inexpensive information and communication technology. The de-institutionalisation, even dismantling, of school systems would be an important feature of the emerging 'network society'. Various cultural, religious and community voices would be powerfully to the fore in the socialisation and learning arrangements for children, some very local in character, others using distance and cross-border networking.
>
> (OECD, 2003, p. 26)

In this scenario the experts at the OECD paint a picture of the emerging influence of a much wider range of players within the education system both locally, via specific community groups, and internationally, by employers and media companies. They describe a more open educational market place in which school systems would be marked by an absence of many of the current governance structures. In this scenario of overlapping and interlocking networks leadership becomes more diffuse marked by what has now become termed 'systems leadership' (Fullan, 2005). These are leaders operating beyond their host organisations exerting influence at various levels within more localised 'mini-systems' and with the capacity to work across these mini-systems. They would therefore be able to effect educational provision not just at the micro level but also at the meso level, by which we mean not just within specific communities but across whole cities and even regions. Each network would be acting as a mini-system capable of delivering a wide range of teaching, engaging in curriculum and materials development, organising community and network resources and managing its own infrastructure and finances.

Many aspects of this scenario have already come into being in parts of the UK where in certain cities and regions large secondary schools, or networks of them, have already become such 'mini-systems'. Although still held within relatively traditional governance structures they are sufficiently powerful to resist a great deal of external influence and have become the dominant 'middle tier' organisation standing between central government and local communities.

The OECD scenarios can be placed along a dimension from re-schooling to de-schooling where at one end of this dimension networks offer possibilities for reforming and improving schools, for example by helping them to become 'core social centres' or extended service schools, and at the other end of this dimension, de-schooling, where networks become the dominant organisational structure for educating and supporting young people, in effect replacing schools.

In the following chapter we set out three scenarios, each outlining a possible direction for how the rise of school networks will affect the education system. We deliberately locate these scenarios within the medium rather than the long term to avoid one of the traps of 'futures thinking' where the proposed scenario seems to offer an almost implausible alternative with little credibility or connection between the current situation and the 'future' presented. Each of our scenarios uses a different lens to examine the possible direction a more networked system might take.

The first scenario focuses on the impact of school networks at the macro or system level, the second focuses on their local impact on the meso or local level within specific communities, and the third on the micro or individual level. Each scenario also attends to a different issue. The first examines networks as a means for providing system coherence by reconnecting school districts/local authorities to schools and central policy; we term this 'reconnecting the middle tier'. The second examines networks as a mechanism to challenge community inequity through the provision of a community's public services, and the third as a vehicle for tackling within-school variation by supporting professional development and the exchange of knowledge. The common theme across all three scenarios is that of connection and reconnection in that networks can provide the leadership, processes and structures that will support effective collective action. In conclusion, we draw on the three scenarios to outline a number of key challenges that must be addressed if the power of networking is to be realised irrespective of the direction travel.

System coherence: networks that reconnect education systems

Many educational systems around the world have been subject to increasing pressures where a relentless drive to raise standards has led to much experimentation and unparalleled levels of policy development causing a centralisation/decentralisation paradox (Ribbins and Burridge, 1994). Here we take England as an example of a system facing such pressures. Historically, in England there was an order to the system, where central policy was transmitted to schools through local government. Within this relationship local government (through the local authority) also had responsibility for providing schools with services ranging from property repairs to the provision of school dinners for children and the professional development of teachers. The close relationship between local authorities and 'their' schools often felt somewhat paternalistic. Some politicians felt this to be a problematic situation. How could one body be responsible for policy implementation, the day-to-day running of schools and providing challenge and support for improvement? In an attempt to drive up standards over the past two decades, successive governments have challenged the very nature of the local authority/school relationship. Central government policies have for the most part freed up schools from local authority control, and local authorities have now become more the commissioner rather than the provider of services. Central to the drive to free up schools has been for government to fund schools directly rather than use the local authority as a conduit for providing resources to schools and to develop mechanisms to hold schools directly accountable to central government.

On the one hand, the decentralisation of resources directly to schools freed them up from local authority control while on the other, it increased their accountability to central government through various mechanisms including a standardised inspection regime. The overall effect within the English system has been the erosion of power of the local authority, which led to a temporary vacuum in the middle tier. Local authorities became streamlined to the point of being under-resourced and found themselves in competition to offer services over which, traditionally, they had a monopoly. However, some local authorities managed to respond quickly to these changes, redefining their relationships with schools and tailoring their provision to their strengths and the needs of schools. For others this was a struggle and relationships deteriorated, and schools began to seek out new sources to commission their services and for a minority, the local authority never had the necessary relationships or services in place, so already schools were looking elsewhere. In addition to dis-empowering local authorities central government set up a range of non-departmental government bodies and actively encouraged the involvement of the private sector, especially in intervening where local authorities were found to be weak or failing. The rise of these new entities within the middle tier has created a complex but largely fragmented landscape, a mono-cultural where the middle tier is seen mainly as a delivery system by central government and is well versed in the official school improvement rhetoric (Thrupp, 2006) of support and challenge. We see local authorities, the National College for School Leadership (NCSL), Specialist Schools and Academies Trust, Tribal, Cambridge Education Associates and other private companies competing for what were traditionally roles and responsibilities assigned to local authorities.

The current situation is one in which jostling for position amongst the middle tier, particularly in terms of access to central government funding and claims to be able to represent schools, means that organisations have developed their own networks of schools on a regional basis around their agendas, a situation which has led to many schools now being part of numerous networks. In a recent survey of schools' network membership carried out as part of our research, schools claimed on average to be part of four networks with some claiming as many as seven. This plurality of overlapping networks may provide a sense of connectivity for the middle tier but at the level of individual schools the benefits of networking have become diluted as school leaders act increasingly instrumentally chasing funding opportunities and access to new ideas and professional development opportunities. In a sense networks have become part of a competitive market not between schools but between middle-tier organisations. In such a climate coordination of efforts across the middle tier becomes problematic. Networks of headteachers struggle to align their efforts with those that focus on the work of departmental heads. Those concerned with curriculum innovation fail to synchronise their work with those involved in professional development. Each of these differing networks will cut across any coordination being attempted by local authorities, many of whom have a limited awareness of what networks actually exist within their locality.

Our emergent scenario is that as school leaders are increasingly exposed to policy makers and the process of policy construction, becoming aware of the power they have within middle-tier organisations and gaining experience of network to network collaboration, then a dramatic shift in the power relationships within this tier will occur. Middle-tier organisations will increasingly become membership organisations in that they will need to respond not only to central government edicts but also to the concerns and aspirations of their members. They will have to do so because of the nature of this membership, which will not be of individual leaders or schools but of networks of schools with clearly articulated visions of the sort of education they wish to provide in their area. These networks will have the ability to form alliances with other networks that share similar concerns and aspirations and in doing so will take on the campaigning characteristics of new social movements. They will form temporary alliances with other networks to achieve large-scale changes within the system. In doing so they will not only set out to meet the needs of their members, the schools and their staff, by providing more bespoke professional development opportunities and new curriculum innovations, they will also change the nature of policy development itself.

We envisage networks forming alliances around issues and concerns that represent their views of worthwhile and effective education rather than those being mandated centrally, as is often the case in the current climate. So for example, one could imagine a scenario where a number of local authority officers, school leaders and policy makers come together around a set of common concerns relating to inclusion. An initial meeting may lead to a joint agreement to meet on a regular basis to develop a coordinated approach of action to tackle these concerns. When this group finds itself in conflict with policies developed centrally it would form alliances with other networks attempting similar innovations and begin to act increasingly politically to change these policies so that they align with the group's efforts.

In the mature version of this scenario, networks operating as social movements would be able to mobilise across the whole system affecting a range of middle-tier organisations and putting increasing pressure on central government. Working in this way would create a campaigning structure where concerted collaborative action would begin to inform policy development to a degree that has been lacking in recent years. Such a process would see issues currently dealt with on the peripheries of the system being drawn into the middle ground as groups of schools start to collaborate on the basis of their religious, educational and political values. These campaigning groups of networks would have the ability to create new structures to access and influence policy makers and political groups and where necessary to collectively resist external influences.

Clearly, such a development would require strong lateral leadership within these educational networks. We would expect to see far more flexibility within network leadership than current conceptualisations allow for. The boundaries between school networks and middle-tier organisations would become fluid as the latter become more reliant upon membership participation. Such fluidity would see individuals increasingly moving between temporary structures created by network alliances and this flow would provide a means of re-connecting different levels of the system. School staff, local authority/middle-tier officers and policy makers may job share or undertake exchange programmes and by doing so increase the range of perspectives and experiences that contribute to policy development and understanding of practice.

Such fluidity would exist between pools or common communities of practice where schools and other agencies join together to form mini-systems, engaging in campaigning for change at the system level. An area where we already see elements of this phenomenon emerging within the current system in the UK is in networks of church schools across diocese. In one sense, here we are arguing for a shift from a series of mini-systems to the emergence of meso-systems, each holding temporary memberships where individuals can opt in or out depending on individual needs, purposes and timing. These meso-systems could add value in a number of areas. First, there would be economies of scale. The combined resources of these systems improve purchasing power of the group and therefore the individuals involved. Second, because of increased connectability there would be enhanced opportunities for the transfer of knowledge and practice, both laterally across and vertically within the system. This scenario erodes the importance of organisational boundaries. This has implications for individual and organisational accountability and autonomy. Increasingly individual leaders become responsible for strands of activity across multiple organisations rather than leaders of activity within single organisations. This has implications for accountability mechanisms. Just as assessing a school's performance on its examination performance becomes nonsensical if students on roll are taught in a number of institutions; it is nonsensical for the work of a leader to be assessed only in one institution if they are working on strands of activity across many schools. Similarly, it would become equally ridiculous to judge a school's performance only on 'their' staff if strands of activity are led by staff from other institutions. It is within contexts such as these that we consider networks to be a possible mechanism serving to reconnect the system and develop an effective middle tier. They would do so by increasing the fluidity of the middle tier at both the 'top' in its connection with central government and at the bottom with its connection to individual schools.

In summary, this first scenario presents a portrait of schools with blurred boundaries but strong network connections that have moved to occupy not only some of the territory currently held by middle-tier organisations but also with the capacity to change the very nature of these organisations. The metaphor we use to describe this change is that the education system moves from an 'atomistic' scenario where schools act as individualised atoms only linked to each other by weak bonds to a 'molecular' scenario where groups of schools are held together by strong bonds. In an atomistic system the middle-tier organisations were required to act as catalysts to coalesce schools and coordinate their working; in the new 'molecular' scenario groups of schools can themselves act as catalysts.

Closing the gap: networks that connect different attempts to challenging social inequity

The second scenario we offer focuses on growing inequity within the education system, specifically the failure to close the gap between the educational achievement and aspirations of pupils from different socio-economic and ethnic groups. Many temporary solutions, including intensive remedial action and the rebranding of schools in some of our most challenging communities have failed to deliver desired changes. Furthermore, policy has persisted with an uncritical approach involving the application and replication of education/ school improvement models across a range of contexts in an attempt to address social issues through education and schools. Increasingly we are recognising that dealing with educational inequality requires reform at the community level beyond schools as organisations. The first signs of this phenomenon are already emerging through innovations such as extended and full-service schools. However, such schools are unlikely to be able to fully compensate for the inequality within the system because of their inability to make effective links with other agencies or key sections of the communities they serve. This is further complicated by the turbulence in both the schools and the communities they serve.

There is a series of important disconnections here that appropriately constituted school networks might overcome. First, there is the disconnection between schools and local communities. Even the subsets of the community that are made up of parents become increasingly distant from schools as their children become older. In some schools this disconnection is compounded by them operating within cultures that are parallel to, rather than part of, the community. These schools offer schooling that is a 'haven' where the students are expected to behave and adhere to an alternative set of values and behaviours to those found within the community. This approach can benefit the students in terms of their experience within school but it can also act as a further barrier between the school and the community. In addition there are the dis-connections between agencies that try to challenge inequality. Although multi-agency approaches are highly fashionable they struggle because they are based on separate organisations, each of which has its own ethos, and because they are populated by professionals with distinct value frameworks and who have spent their careers being enculturated into different professional cultures and whose individual professional networks rarely cross the boundaries between agencies. Finally, there is the disconnection between the different overarching strategies for overcoming inequality. Urban regeneration programmes run over different time frames and operate in different localities than strategies focusing on employment, health, civic engagement and business development. In this environment much of the energy associated with these innovations becomes dissipated and funding that could be spent in local communities goes to supporting external professionals who leave once the funding runs out.

Our emergent scenario would be one in which multiple initiatives are coordinated by school networks that act as a reservoir of knowledge, capacity and funding. We see a blurring of organisational and professional boundaries in an attempt to provide systematic efforts to invest in localities. This scenario takes us beyond the use of interim organisations to where networks of schools have redefined their relationship with the local community and local professionals. This emergent scenario still presents networks as acting as medium-term palliatives to the disconnected nature of initiatives and fragmented professional agendas. The mature scenario would see a radically different approach.

In the mature scenario school networks will have developed to the point where they have established a strong local identity capable of providing a counterbalance to the range of professional identities that cause such issues in current attempts to encourage more multi-agency working. These identities would reflect not only the professionals engaged in the network but also would be rooted within the localities they serve. Networks would develop this sense of identity by becoming providers of initial training for a range of professionals, building on current approaches to teacher training within schools. Professionals would be encultured into a local identity that would be interwoven into the construction of their professional identities. This approach would start to overcome the main paradox of multi-agency working, in that we train and develop professionals separately: they build their professional networks within separate organisations, we then give them performance targets that are not interdependent, and then ask these fragmented groups of professionals to work together. In this mature scenario school networks become integrated into the 'locality', networks generating training programmes for local people who would become increasingly represented within the services that support them, mediating and brokering a wide range of initiatives so that capacity is built within the locality rather than being dissipated, and creating an inclusive educational and social reform agenda with local communities rather than imposing one upon them.

This second scenario presents not only a more heterogeneous form of leadership, involving a range of leaders from diverse backgrounds, but also a more expansive notion of what it means to be an educational leader. To effectively engage with a challenge such as social inequity means engaging with issues beyond schools and recognising not only the importance of family and communities in support of in-school learning but also the connection between in-school and out-of-school learning. This form of locality leadership relies on an offer of networked educational provision that originates as much outside the schools system as within it. Rather than being a 'headteacher' of a school with some understanding of social work, community development and third-sector organisations, these network leaders will have extensive experience of leading in this specific locality. As such they will need to have a local provenance, a deep understanding and connection with their locality and the capabilities and capacities of the services and community organisations within it. They would have to be leaders capable of engaging the local community as much as local professionals and as such might have to adopt leadership approaches that are valued within the local community. Unless the network is able to build a strong shared local identity there could be a number of leadership challenges in how to reconcile what might be very different expectations of what it means to be a leader between professionals and community members.

This scenario will not fit easily within those current discussions of educational leadership that treat leadership as arising purely from competence and disconnected from context and notions of self. Issues such as a lack of trust in schools and scepticism about what they can achieve from those who they have already failed mean that locality leadership will rely heavily upon local leaders. That is leaders who have strong connections with a given place, who can use their social and professional connections to make things happen, and who already have a degree of trust within local communities. Previously we have talked about the power of school networks to shift the mindset of educationalists from an individualised to a collective responsibility. In this scenario we are talking about developing this sense of collective responsibility outwards from schools to whole communities, so that they become committed as a whole to the education of 'their' children.

Within-school variation: networks that connect individual and school improvement

England, like other western societies, suffers from wide variation within schools. This may seem a strange starting place for a scenario where school-based networks are the focus of within-school variation. However, if we think about networks as a framing device for supporting individual learning by enhancing the opportunities for professional networking, they become a possible and logical solution for this issue. There have been a range of research projects on leadership and continuing professional development that have stressed the role played by social and professional networks in providing support, maintaining commitment and providing positive professional identities for teachers (Fullan, 1991). In parallel with these types of studies there has been research that has shown how individuals can be drawn in through these individual social networks into more formalised learning opportunities and leadership experiences (Jervis-Tracey, 2005). The thrust of our argument is that school-based networks can offer the individual teacher two key forms of networking, which when integrated are sufficiently powerful to significantly reduce within-school variation, an observation based on Lee Schulman's (1987) work on teachers' knowledge bases. Schulman's argument is that at the centre of the craft of teaching is the ability to find the optimal combination of pedagogy and content for a particular group of students so they find it engaging and appropriate for their current level of understanding. Our arguments are based on the assumption that one of the major causes of within-school variation is discrepancies in both teachers' subject and pedagogic knowledge that limit their ability to optimise their integration and therefore construct powerful learning experiences.

Our emergent scenario would be a network-based solution that helped individual teachers to develop cross-school subject-based networks that enhanced their understanding of subject matter, and to integrate these with within-school networking that supported their development of effective pedagogical approaches. Clearly knowledge of effective pedagogies can be gained through cross-school networking but the highly contextualised form of this knowledge that teachers value is that which 'works with their children in their school'. Any cross-school networking would therefore need to be with similar children in a similar context. In this scenario what is required is a combination of individual networks that support both greater pedagogical and content understanding. This notion of integrated networks lies at the heart of our response to within-school variation.

In this scenario the purpose of school-based networks is to support and enhance egocentric professional learning networks. Support could be in a number of forms, for example by contributing expertise to the design of key processes such as mentoring and coaching and joint planning in specific curriculum areas. In England aspects of this emerging scenario are already present within the system through subject-specific associations (e.g. Association of Science Educators), networks of schools (e.g. Specialist Schools and Academies Trust) and individual school attempts to improve teaching and learning. However, to date these efforts tend to be fragmented and evolve on an ad hoc basis. Furthermore, historically there has been very little interplay between whole-school reform initiatives based on particular pedagogies or curriculum development models and subject specific networks. So we believe the most pressing challenge is to develop our understanding of how school networks can relate to individual professional networking.

A key leadership challenge for this latticing of developments in pedagogy and content is the requirement for different forms of leadership within and across organisational boundaries, requiring different knowledge and expertise. Our impression from our own work is that few schools experiencing wide variations in their pupils' and teachers' performance have this knowledge and expertise in place in sufficient quantities. Again this becomes a key role for the broader school network in supporting individual learning by providing additional leadership capacity. As long as individual schools have enough capacity to put some structures and processes in place so that they can make use of the network's expertise and leadership capacity, this approach should be able to take hold. However, for a minority of schools the internal capacity or conditions may need working on before attempting to implement such an approach. For schools with individualised or balkanised cultures (Hargreaves, 1994), it is unlikely that within-school networking will be easy or successful. In such circumstances the external school network can be drawn on to work with some enthusiasts in order to 'kick start' action and challenge resistant cultures. Again, our experience suggests that over time this approach can break down resistance. External networking supports the development of a culture that values internal collaboration, creating a critical mass who are willing and able to engage. At this stage the school is ready for both within- and between-school networking.

The three scenarios outlined above use the lenses of macro, meso and micro change to outline the potential of networks to support development and change across the system, within local communities and at the level of individual teaching practice. With this in mind, we conclude by reflecting on three challenges that permeate through all scenarios. It is our view that if we are to realise the potential of school-based networks these challenges require further attention in terms of research and policy development.

Constitution

The first of our three key challenges relates to the constitution of networks. By this we mean the mix and balance of constituent parts and members of the network and how they come together as a formal entity. At the core of this issue is the dilemma between conscription and volunteerism. We know most successful networks usually involve volunteers who choose to initiate or join the network. The weakness of this approach is those schools with potentially the most to gain may decide networking is not for them. We have found this is often the case with schools facing challenging circumstances, especially in those who feel overwhelmed by the pace of change and need to manage multiple initiatives and interventions. This is also an issue for coasting schools who perceive themselves as high performing and therefore do not think they will benefit from involvement and consequently view networking as a low priority activity. There are also arguments within network theory about the advantages of heterogeneous versus homogeneous membership profiles, particularly with respect to levels of capacity, perceived expertise and relative levels of performance.

The alternative, conscription, is problematic even when there is good reason and the benefits are clearly articulated. For example issues of equity and inclusion are often used to justify 'putting' schools into a particular network. Unfortunately although network membership can be mandated, meaningful participation cannot. When individuals and organisations are coerced into networks, they tend to be hollow or empty with little chance of sustaining themselves beyond any incentives or inducements.

The issue here is that networks are no more likely than other organisational forms to overcome organisational inequalities. Networks are just as capable as acting as monopolies drawing down greater funding than individual schools and exerting unfair influence on local education systems. How then as we progress to a more networked landscape do we ensure that networks do not reinforce existing inequalities?

Relationships

The second key challenge we want to highlight relates to the importance of relationships, a core theme running through this book. Much attention has been paid to the nature of relationships and what underpins them. Within a networking context we argue that trust is the key driver of positive relationships. Trust is both the lubricant and the glue of relationships. On one hand trust can allow slippage and flexibility by oiling situations. For example, in trusting relationships individuals are more likely to be generous and compromises are more likely to be negotiated. On the other hand trust acts as a force binding individuals, and indeed organisations, together. For example, in times of crisis if people trust each other they are more likely to stand together and face the situation collectively. Where trust is limited people are more likely to revert to a pessimistic perspective and protect their own resources and territory.

One of the key paradoxes of networks is that people prefer to work with people they already know and trust while some of the greatest gains of networking require that you reach out to others and form new collaborations that fulfil unmet needs and help support new approaches. The challenge here is how to build sufficient trust within education systems so that school networks become a force for inclusion rather than exclusion and do not encourage parochialism.

Purpose and identity

The third key challenge we outline is concerned with purpose and identity. By this we mean the purpose of the network, in terms of its aims and objectives, and the identity of the individuals within the network, who they are and where they locate themselves. In England, many networks have emerged from opportunities provided by central government. For example, the Leadership Incentive Grant (LIG) provided schools with resources to develop leadership capacity through collaboration. Others have developed from the desire to reject or subvert externally imposed change or to tackle a localised problem, issue or crisis. The purposes of school-based networks are incredibly varied, ranging from school improvement networks, curriculum development networks, professional development networks to multi-agency and community-based networks.

In terms of identity, the challenge rests within the nature of those involved within the network. Homogeneous school-based networks of teachers are the least problematic, as they involve only teachers and therefore there will be at least some consensus in terms of understanding and perspective. However, we only have to think of a staffroom and its characters to recognise the diversity of values, approach and practice within a school. In a network setting you have to add teachers versed in a range of school cultures, with different professional experiences from organisations at various stages of development, and it quickly becomes clear that the idea of one 'teacher' identity is flawed and in reality there will be a number of contrasting individual identities working at different levels. The situation becomes far more complex when networks involve working across professional boundaries.

If school-based networks are to reach their potential we need to break down barriers and think beyond schools and education. An ambitious move might be to challenge the orthodoxy of leadership identity by changing the initial training of professionals and their continuous professional development by creating learning contexts that counterbalance strong professional identities with those based on locality. The challenge here is to reconceptualise educational leadership in terms of generating and transferring knowledge, trust and shared purposes and identities at various levels across education systems and local communities.

References

Ainscow, M., Muijs, D. and West, M. (2006) 'Collaboration as a strategy for improving schools in challenging circumstances'. *Improving Schools* 9 (3) November: 192–202.

Barge, J. K. (1996) 'Leadership skills and the dialectics of leadership in group decision making'. In Hirowaka, R. and Poole. M. (eds) *Communication and Group Decision Making*. Thousand Oaks, CA: Sage.

Bell, L., Bolam, R. and Cubillo, L. (2006) *A Systematic Review of the Impact of School Leadership and Management on Student Outcomes*. London: Eppi-Centre, Social Science Research Unit, Institute of Education.

Berliner, B. (1997) 'What it takes to work together: the promise of educational partnerships'. *Knowledge Brief* 14: 2–7.

Bryk, A., Camburn, E. and Seashore, L. K. (1999) 'Professional community in Chicago elementary schools: facilitating factors and organizational consequences'. *Educational Administration Quarterly* 35 (5): 751–781.

Burbules, N. and Densmore, K. (1991) 'The limits of making teaching a profession'. *Education Policy* 5 (1): 44–63.

Burke, R. (2005) *Brokerage and Closure: An Introduction to Social Capital*. Oxford: Oxford University Press.

Burt, R. S. (2001) 'Bandwith and echo: trust information, and gossip in social networks'. In Casella, A. and Rauch, J. (eds) *Networks and Markets*. New York: Sage, pp. 30–74.

Branch, J., Smith, B., Cannon, J. and Bedingham, K. (1995) 'Building a consortium alliance for learning – the Volvo experience'. *Journal of European Industrial Training* 19 (1): 18–23.

Callinicos, A. (1987) *Making History: Agency Structure and Change in Social Theory*. Oxford: Polity Press.

Campbell, A., Kane, I., Keating, I., Cockett, K., McConnell, A. and Baxter, C. (2005) *Networked Learning Communities and Higher Education Links Project: Interim Report*. Nottingham: NCSL.

Castells, M. (2001) *The Internet Galaxy*. Oxford: Oxford University Press.

Chapman, C. (2006) *School Improvement Through External Intervention?* London: Continuum.

Chapman, C. and Fullan, M. (2007) 'Collaboration and partnership for equitable improvement: towards a networked learning system?' *School Leadership and Management* 27 (3): 205–211.

Chapman, C., Allen, T. and Harris, A. (2004) *Networked Learning Communities and Schools Facing Challenging Circumstances*. Warwick: University of Warwick.

Chapman, C., Lindsay, G. and Harris, A. (2006) Collaborative Reform for Schools in Difficulty (Symposium), American Educational Research Association annual meeting, San Francisco, 7–11 April.

Chapman, C., Ainscow, M., Bragg, J., Gunter, H., Hull, J., Mongon, D., Muijs, D. and West, M. (2008) *Emerging Patterns of School Leadership: Current Trends and Future Directions*. Nottingham: NCSL.

Church, M., Bitel, M., Armstrong, K., Fernando, P., Gould, H., Joss, S., Marwaha-Diedrich, M., Torre, A. L. D. L. and Vouhé, C. (2002) *Participation, Relationships and Dynamic Change: New Thinking on Evaluating the Work of International Networks*. London: University College London.

Coburn, C. (2003) 'Rethinking scale: moving beyond numbers to deep and lasting change'. *Educational Researcher* 32: 3–12.

Cordingley, P., Bell, M., Rundell, B. and Evans, D. (2003) *The Impact of Collaborative CPD on Classroom Teaching and Learning*. London: Eppi-Centre, Social Science Research Unit, Institute of Education.

CRC (Center for Research on the Context of Teaching) (2002) *Bay Area School Reform Collaborative: Phase One (1996–2001)*. Stanford, CA: Stanford University CRC.

Day, C. and Hadfield, M. (2004) 'Learning through networks: partnerships and the power of action research'. *Educational Action Research: An International Journal* 12: 575–586.

Day, C., Harris, A., Hadfield, M., Tolley, H. and Beresford, J. (2000) *Leading Schools in Times of Change*. Buckingham: Open University Press.

Deloitte & Touche (2000) *Evaluation of European School Partnerships under Comenius Action 1 & Lingua Action E*. July. London: Deloitte & Touche.

Dyson, A. (2006) 'Beyond the school gates: context, disadvantage and "urban schools"'. In Ainscow, M. and West, M. (eds) *Improving Urban School: Leadership and Collaboration*. Buckingham: Open University Press, pp. 130–144.

Fielding, M. (1999) 'Radical collegiality: affirming teaching as an inclusive professional practice'. *Australian Educational Researcher* 26: 1–34.

Fullan, M. (1991) *The New Meaning of Educational Change*. London: Cassell.

Fullan, M. (2005) *Leadership and Sustainability: System Thinkers in Action*. Thousand Oaks, CA: Corwin Press.

Giddens, A. (1994) *Beyond Left and Right: The Future of Radical Politics*. Oxford: Polity Press.

Hadfield, M. (2005) 'Middle leaders and the nature of distributed leadership in networks'. Paper presented at American Educational Research Association (AERA) Conference, Montreal, 11–15 April 2004.

Hadfield, M. (2007) 'Co-leaders and middle leaders: the dynamic between leaders and followers in networks of schools'. *School Leadership and Management* 27: 259–283.

Hadfield, M. and Jopling, M. (2007) *The Potential of Collaboratives to Support Schools in Complex and Challenging Circumstances*. Nottingham: NCSL.

Hadfield, M., Jopling, M., Noden, C., O'Leary, D. and Stott, A. (2005) *The Impact of Networking and Collaboration: The Existing Knowledge-base*. Nottingham: NCSL Innovation Unit.

Hadfield, M., Chapman, C., Curryer, I. and Barret, P. (2002) *Building Capacity Developing Your School*. Nottingham: NCSL.

Hadfield, M., Noden, C., Stott, A., McGregor, J. and Anderson, M. (2004a) 'The leadership of adult learning in school networks'. *Report of the Network Learning Communities Programme Inquiry 2004.* Nottingham: NCSL.

Hadfield, M., Spender, B., Holmes, D. and Bavington, T. (2004b) Leading Networks: The Dynamic between Processes and Structures. What Works? The annual meeting of the American Educational Research Association, San Diego.

Hargreaves, A. (1994) *Changing Teachers, Changing Times: Teachers' Work and Culture in the Postmodern Age.* New York: Teachers College Press.

Hargreaves, A. and Fink, D. (2004) 'The seven principles of sustainable leadership'. *Educational Leadership* 16 (7): 8–14.

Hargreaves, A. and Fullan, M. (1992) *Teacher Development and Educational Change.* New York: Falmer Press.

Hargreaves, D. (2003) *Education Epidemic: Transforming Secondary Schools Through Innovation Networks.* London: Demos.

Hersey, P., Blanchard, K. H. and Johnson, D. (2001) *Management of Organizational Behaviour: Leading Human Resources.* Englewood Cliffs, NJ: Prentice Hall.

Hopkins, D. (2000) *Schooling for Tomorrow: Innovation and Networks.* OECD/SERI seminar, Lisbon, 14–15 September.

Hopkins, D. and Lagerweij, N. (1996) 'The school improvement knowledge base'. In Reynolds, D., Bollen, R., Creemers, B., Hopkins, D., Stoll, L. and Lagerweij, L. (eds) *Making Good Schools – Linking School Effectiveness and School Improvement.* London: Routledge, pp. 59–93.

Hudson-Ross, S. (2001) 'Intertwining opportunities: participants' perceptions of professional growth within a multiple-site teacher education network at the secondary level'. *Teaching and Teacher Education* 17 (4): 433–454.

Jackson, D. (2005) 'Capacity, capacity building and capacity utilisation: implications for reform'. Unpublished report. Milton Keynes: Network Learning Communities Programme.

Jackson, D. and Payne, G. (2003) *Reflections – Learning Themes from the First Nine Months of the Networked Learning Communities Programme.* Nottingham: NCSL.

Jervis-Tracey, P. (2005) 'Inter-institutional networks and alliances: new directions in leadership'. *International Journal of Leadership in Education* 8 (4): 291–308.

Kerr, D., Aiston, S., White, K., Holland, M. and Grayson, H. (2003) *Review of Networked Learning Communities.* Nottingham: NCSL.

Lieberman, A. (1996) 'Creating intentional learning communities'. *Educational Leadership* 54 (3): 51–55.

Lieberman, A. (1999) 'Networks'. *Journal of Staff Development* 20 (2): 43–44.

Lieberman, A. and Grolnick, M. (1996) 'Networks and reform in American education'. *Teacher's College Record* 98: 1–44.

Lieberman, A. and Wood, D. (2004) 'Untangling the threads: networks, community and teacher learning in the national writing projects'. In McCarthy, H., Miller, P. and Skidmore P. (eds) *Network Logic: Who Governs in an Interconnected World?* London: Demos, pp. 63–76.

Little, J. W. (1993) *Teachers' Professional Development in an Era of Reform.* New York: National Center for Restructuring Education, Schools and Teaching.

McGregor, J. and Fielding, M. (2005) Deconstructing Student Voice: New Spaces for Dialogue or New Opportunities for Surveillance? American Education Research Association (AERA) conference, Montreal.

McLaughlin, M. and Talbert, J. (2006) *Building School-based Teacher Learning Communities*. New York: Teachers College Press.

Mandell, M. (1999) 'Community collaborations: working through network structures'. *Policy Studies Review* 16 (1): 42–65.

Mitchell, C. and Sackney, L. (2000) *Profound Improvement: Building Capacity for a Learning Community*. Lisse, The Netherlands: Swets & Zeitlinger.

MORI (2004) *Mori Teachers' Omnibus 2004* (Wave 3). London: MORI.

MSSC (Manchester and Salford Schools Consortium) (2006) *Summary of Final Report 2006*. Manchester: MSCC.

Newell, S. and Swan, J. (2000) 'Trust and inter-organizational networking'. *Human Relations* 53 (10): 1287–1328.

NLC Annual Inquiry Report (2004) Unpublished report. Nottingham: NCSL.

NLG (2005) *International Perspectives on Networked Learning*. Nottingham: NLG.

Nooteboom, B. (2007) 'Social capital, institutions and trust'. *Review of Social Economy* 65 (1): 29–53.

Oberschall, A. (1973) *Social Conflict and Social Movements*. Englewood Cliffs, NJ: Prentice Hall.

OECD (2003) 'Networks of innovation: towards new models for managing schools and systems'. *Schooling for Tomorrow*. Paris: OECD.

OfSTED (2003) *Excellence in Cities and EAZs, Management and Impact*. London: OfSTED.

PWC (PriceWaterhouseCoopers) (2007) *Independent Study into School Leadership*. London: DfES.

Reyes, P. and Phillips, J. (2002) 'Annenberg evaluation report: lessons learned on urban school reform'. *Houston Annenberg Challenge Research and Evaluation Study*. Austin, TX: The University of Texas.

Ribbins, P. and Burridge, E. (1994) *Improving Education: Promoting Quality in Schools*. London: Cassell.

Rudd, P., Holland, M., Sanders, D., Massey, A. and White, G. (2004) *An Evaluation of the Beacon Schools Initiative*. Slough: NFER.

Ruddock, J., Berry, M., Brown, N. and Frost, D. (2000) 'Schools learning from other schools: co-operation in a climate of competition'. *Research Papers in Education* 15: 259–274.

Sachs, J. (2000) 'The activist professional'. *Journal of Educational Change* 1 (1) January: 77–95.

Sammons, P., Mujtaba, T., Earl, L. and Gu, Qing (2007) 'Participation in network learning community programmes and standards of pupil achievement: does it make a difference?' *School Leadership and Management* 27 (3): 213–238.

Schulman, L. (1987) 'Knowledge and teaching: foundations of the new reforms'. *Harvard Educational Review* 57 (1): 1–22.

Sergiovanni, T. (2001) *The Principalship: A Reflective Practice Perspective*. Fourth edition. Boston: Allyn and Bacon.

Sheppard, B. and Tuchinsky, M. (1996) 'Micro-ob and the network organisation'. In Kramer, R. and Tyler T. (eds) *Trust in Organisations*. Thousand Oaks, CA: Sage, pp. 140–165.

Skidmore, P. (2004) 'Leading between: leadership and trust in a network society'. *Network Logic*. London: Demos.

Sliwka, A. (2003) 'Networking for educational innovation: a comparative analysis'. In *Networks of Innovation: Towards New Models for Managing Schools and Systems*. Paris: OECD, pp. 49–63.

Snow, D. A., Rochford, E. B., Worden, S. K. and Benford, R. D. (1986) 'Frame alignment processes, micromobilization and movement participation'. *American Sociological Review* 51: 464–481.

Somekh, B. (1994) 'Inhabiting each other's castles: towards knowledge and mutual growth through collaboration'. *Educational Action Research* 2 (3): 357–381.

Starkey, P. (1997) *Networking for Development, International Forum for Rural Transport and Development*. London: International Forum for Rural Transport and Development.

Stott, A., Jopling, M. and Kilcher, A. (2006) *How Do School-to-School Networks Work?* Nottingham: NCSL.

Sullivan, H. and Skelcher, C. (2003) *Working Across Boundaries: Collaboration in Public Services*. Basingstoke: Palgrave Macmillan.

Tell, J. (2000) 'Learning networks – a metaphor for inter organizational development in SMEs'. *Enterprise and Innovation Management Studies* 1 (3): 303–317.

Thrupp, M. (2006) *School Improvement: An Unofficial Approach*. London: Continuum.

Toole, J. and Louis, K. S. (2002) 'The role of professional learning communities in international education'. In Leithwood, K. and Hallinger, P. (eds) *Second International Handbook of Educational Leadership and Administration*. Dordrecht: Kluwer.

Wohlstetter, P. and Smith, A. K. (2000) 'A different approach to systemic reform: network structures in Los Angeles'. *Phi Delta Kappan* 87 (7): 508–515.

Wohlstetter, P., Malloy, C. L., Chau, D. and Polhemus, J. L. (2003) 'Improving schools through networks: a new approach to urban school reform'. *Educational Policy* 17: 399–430.

Woods, P. A. and Woods, G. J. (2004) 'Modernizing leadership through private participation: a marriage of inconvenience with public ethos?' *Journal of Educational Policy* 19 (6): 643–672.

Woods, R. and Hadfield, M. (2006) *What Are We Learning About Sustaining Networks of Schools?* Nottingham: NCSL.

Index